Contents

Acknowledgements

The authors and publishers acknowledge the following sources of copyright material and are grateful for the permissions granted. While every effort has been made, it has not always been possible to identify the sources of all the material used, or to trace all copyright holders. If any omissions are brought to our notice, we will be happy to include the appropriate acknowledgements on reprinting.

pp.3-6: 'The Seal Wife' retold by Jenny Tod, from *A World of Folk Tales*, ed. Sue Stewart © Scottish Cultural Press, 1996 www.scottishbooks.com; pp.7-21: *Out of Bounds* by Beverley Naidoo (Puffin, 2001) © Beverley Naidoo, 2001; p.22-31: 'Mr Naidoo's Hundredth Birthday 'from *An Eye for Colour* (Faber and Faber, 1991) © Norman Silver; pp.32-4: 'Life for Us', 'The Middle Way', 'My Children' by Choman Hardi, from *Life for Us* (Bloodaxe Books, 2004), www.bloodaxebooks.com; pp.35-9: 'Robert and the Dog' from *A Forest of Flowers* by Ken Saro-Wiwa © Ken Saro-Wiwa, reproduced by permission of Pearson Education and Saros International Publishers; pp.40-47: 'In the Name of My Father' by Ken Wiwa from the *Observer*, Sunday, 6 November 2005 © Ken Wiwa, reproduced by permission of the author; pp.48-53: 'A Place to Call Home' by Simon Armitage from *All Points North* (Viking, 1998) © Simon Armitage, 1998; pp.64-6: 'The Hunting of Death' by Geraldine McCaughrean from *Golden Myths and Legends of the World* (Orion Children's Books, a division of The Orion Publishing Group Ltd, 1999), reproduced by permission; pp.67-9: 'Cassien's Story' by Cassien Mbanda, reproduced by permission of SURF; pp.70-2: 'Snipers' by Roger McGough from *Watchwords* (© Roger McGough, 1969) is reproduced by permission of PFD (www.pfd.co.uk) on behalf of Roger McGough; pp.73-88: 'Cut Me, and I Bleed Khaki' by Terence Blacker from *Like Father Like Son*' ed. Tony Bradman (Kingfisher, 2006) © Terence Blacker; pp.89-106: 'Barefoot Gen' by Keiji Nakazawa from *Manga Manga: The World of Japanese Comics* by Frederik L Schodt and Osama Tezuka, reproduced by permission of Last Gasp, www.lastgasp.com; pp.107-8: 'Enola Gay' by Esther Morgan, reproduced by permission of the author; pp.109-13: 'Homage' by Nadine Gordimer from *Loot and Other Stories*, reproduced by permission of A P Watt Ltd on behalf of Felix Licensing BV, Penguin Group (Canada) and Russell & Volkening Inc; pp.125-30: extract from *Zlata's Diary: A Child's Life in Sarajevo* by Zlata Filipović, translated by Christina Pribichevich-Zorić (Viking, 1994), first published in France as *'Le Journal de Zlata'* by Fixot et Editions Robert Laffont 1993, Copyright © Fixot et Editions Robert Laffont, 1993, reproduced by permission of Penguin Books Ltd and Susanna Lea Associates on behalf of the author; pp.131–33: 'Cruelty to Children' by R. K. Narayan, from *Story Teller's World,* reproduced by permission of Penguin Books India; pp.134–36: 'Guess Who is Coming to Dinner' by Darija Stojnić from *The Silver Throat of the Moon: Writing in Exile,* ed. Jennifer Langer, 2005, reproduced by permission of Five Leaves Publications; pp.137–42: 'The Mailed Parcel' by Ibrahim Ahmed from *The Silver Throat of the Moon: Writing in Exile,* ed. Jennifer Langer, 2005, reproduced by permission of Five Leaves Publications; pp.143–55: 'Power' by Jack Cope from *Stories from Central and Southern Africa,* reprinted by permission of Harcourt Education; pp.156–62: 'How to Beat the System' by Robert West from *Out of the Night: Writings from Death Row,* ed. Marie Mulvey Roberts with Benjamin Zephaniah (New Clarion Press, 1994); pp.173–84: 'Film Boy' by Alexander McCall Smith from *Stories of the World* compiled by Federation of Children's Book Groups; pp.185–95: 'First Confession' by Frank O'Connor from *Collected Stories* ed. Richard Ellmann, Joan Daves Agency on behalf of the author; p.196: 'I Like to Stay Up' from *Poetry Jump-Up* by Grace Nichols © Grace Nichols, 1984, reproduced by permission of Curtis Brown Group Ltd; pp.197–98: extract from *Whole of a Morning Sky* by Grace Nichols (Virago Press Ltd, 1986), reproduced by permission of Little, Brown Book Group; pp. 199–201: 'Night of the Scorpion' by Nissim Ezekiel, from *Poetry Jump-Up,* ed. Grace Nichols (Puffin, 1990), reproduced by permission of Oxford University Press India, New Delhi; pp.202–10: 'The Long Trial' by Andrée Chedid from *Unwinding Threads: Writings by Women in Africa,* reprinted by permission of Harcourt Education; pp.211–24: extract from *The Storyteller's Daughter: Return to a Lost Homeland* by Saira Shah (Michael Joseph, 2003) © Saira Shah, 2002.

The publishers would like to thank the following for permission to reproduce photgraphs: p.4: Scottish Island © Travel Scotland – Paul White/Alamy; p.40 (*l*): Ken Saro Wiwa, Sutton-Hibbert/Rex Features; p.40 (*r*): Ken Wiwa, Times Newspapers/Rex Features; p.67: Cassien Mbanda, reproduced by permission of SURF; p.88: Military man © Angie Sharp/Alamy; p.89: Atom Bomb Hiroshima, PA Photos; p.108: Enola Gay crew © Ho/epa/Corbis; p.144 – Pylons © Jen Nieth/zefa/Corbis; p.162 – Death Row © Christian Schmidt/zefa/Corbis.

General introduction

Take another look at the front cover of this book. Most young people in the UK today are touched by the multi-cultural mix that is the basis of modern music: the sounds and beats of reggae, jazz, hip-hop, rap, classical and world music blend and build to create new tunes for a modern generation. Some people like to focus on the lyrics and notice how they reflect the concerns of our society, whether they are meditations on love and relationships or more hard-hitting political protest on issues like war and violence.

In the mix is a collection of non-fiction, fiction and poetry that celebrates just this: the way our society, our selves and our views are built and enriched by a wide variety of cultures. Just like music, literature is shaped by its cultural context and its historical roots.

Some of the texts emphasise the shared experience of humanity – that despite our cultural differences our concerns, relationships and reactions to events are alike. The section on 'People and relationships' will introduce you to some interesting and bizarre people, and encourage you to think about their psychology and your personal response.

Other texts focus on what is particular about a culture: for example, the poet Grace Nichols remembers the ghost or 'jumbie' stories told in Guyana during her childhood, while Alexander McCall Smith writes about the Bollywood film world of India. These texts can be found in the section on 'Cultural traditions'.

This collection also includes some thought-provoking and shocking texts. Many of these touch on political issues to do with war, imprisonment, death and violence. Teenagers of my generation, growing up in the 1980s in 'Thatcher's Britain', were accused of being politically lazy; at times I've preferred to bury my head in the sand about this kind of topic. How true do you think this is of your generation? Researching this book has really shaken me into thinking about the violence that occurs in our world in the name of politics and religion. I hope you are as stimulated as I have been by hearing how people survive and react in brutal situations. You'll find a piece of autobiography from a boy who survived the genocide in Rwanda; a Japanese comic that describes the events of an atomic bomb dropped on Hiroshima; advice for teenagers from a murderer sentenced to death in America; and a son's thoughts on the political murder of his father in Nigeria.

It is not only imprisonment and political oppression that can silence the human voice. As more people move from one country to another to make new lives as refugees and exiles, I wanted to include some of these new voices writing in English. Many writers who are forced to leave their countries also leave behind the most precious tool of their trade, their language. There is writing here from Iraq, Kurdistan and Bosnia, representing authors who have had to relearn their trade in a new tongue. These stories will give you the chance to understand something of the refugee experience and the importance of openness and compassion in our society.

The texts are arranged in four sections, with the more difficult ones placed at the end of the section. To support your reading, certain words (these are numbered) in the texts are explained in the footnotes. Ideas for further reading accompany each text. Each section concludes with a range of reading, writing, speaking, listening and drama activities to help you explore and enjoy the authors' ideas, opinions, style, language and techniques. Through this exploration you will, I hope, gain an insight into what makes a good text work, in terms of its structure and content, and think about what we can learn from the situations people find themselves in. Many of the texts will touch on issues you are also addressing in the wider curriculum, through History, PSHE and Enrichment. The text-specific activities pages are divided into the following activity types: *Before you read* (pre-reading stimulation activities), *What's it about?* (comprehension-style questions) and *Thinking about the text* (activities which move beyond the text itself). At the very end of each section, a series of *Compare and contrast* activities provide opportunities to compare two or more texts.

My main concern in selecting these texts was that they should be excellent pieces of writing that you will enjoy. I hope they provoke lively discussions and help you to understand more about who we are and where we come from in today's global community.

Esther Menon

1 People and relationships

Meeting people from around the world can be an enriching experience: it allows us to learn more about other cultures, to find similarities and differences in viewpoints and experiences, and to build friendships. Such relationships can encourage us to question our own beliefs and ways of life and to adjust the way we see things. Family and friendship are basic human needs. The texts in this section show how there can be similarities and differences in the way these needs are met throughout the world.

Activities

1   Think about the people who have played an important role in your life. Copy the diagram below and write down a person's name in each of the boxes. Add some notes about each person, then choose one or two to discuss with a partner.

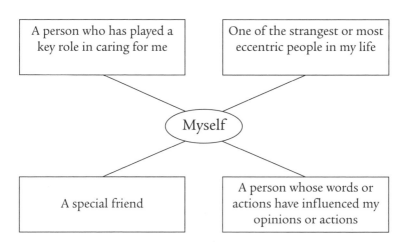

2   What does the term 'the family' mean and what is its role in the society you live in?

   a   Discuss the question above with the rest of your class and agree on a definition of 'the family' and its function.

   b   The role of the family can be slightly different in different countries. Can you think of any other cultures for which your agreed definition would need to be altered?

3   You might have seen the film *Sleepless in Seattle*. Sam (played by Tom Hanks) is a widower and his young son advertises on the radio for a new wife for his father and a mother for himself. You can watch the trailer at http://movies2.nytimes.com/movie/45166/Sleepless-in-Seattle/trailer

Write a script for your own advert or podcast for a new person in your life. Choose one of the roles below. Think carefully about the qualities you would want the person to have.
- Husband/Wife
- Partner
- Grandparent
- Father
- Best friend
- Step-parent

The Seal Wife (Scotland)

retold by Jenny Tod

This story from Scotland is a folk tale. Here it is retold by Jenny Tod, but various different versions of the story exist because of the way folk tales have been passed on orally from one generation to another. Transformation, where a person changes their physical form, is a common theme in folk tales.

A long, long time ago, the Atlantic Sea surrounding the northern and western isles off the mainland of Scotland was filled with the song and laughter of mermaids. These were the children of the King and Queen of the sea. They had bodies just like our own when they came onto dry land and, when they were in the water, their legs and feet would become as a fish's tail. Mermaids enjoyed life. Their long hair flowed with the waves as they raced the tides in and out to sea. Their eyes danced with the joys of sparkling phosphorescence.[1]

When the Queen of the sea died, the lonely King remarried, but his new wife became jealous of the beauty and happiness of her stepchildren. She collected poisonous berries from the sea floor and gave them to each child to eat. Slowly the mermaids' arms and legs were changed to flippers. A thick, furry grey skin grew over their entire bodies. All that remained of their former selves was their large, now wistful, dark brown eyes. The mermaids were changed to selkies (seals).

Full moon, you may know, has very strong powers. It happened that, for the selkies, from sunset to sunrise of each full moon the poisonous berry lost its curse. They could come ashore for this short time, with human limbs once more. As the sun rose in the morning, the pull of the tide would call them back to their seal life in the deep, cold seas.

---

[1]**phosphorescence**   luminous quality

Each month, as the full moon rose from the ocean and shone its light across the seas, the selkies would again dance and sing on the rocky and sandy shores of the west.

One such night a fisherlad had been out to set his creels and was pulling his boat up the shingly shore when he heard laughter nearby. He made his way in the glow of the moonlight over the rocks toward the next bay. There, just below him, dancing naked and joyful on the still wet sand, was a gathering of the most beautiful boys and girls he had ever seen.

This moment of wonder lasted for ever and for a few seconds. The fisherlad realized he was witnessing the rare sight of selkie children on land. He knew they were the shyest creatures on earth, and that if he disturbed them they would leap into the waves. He knew theirs was a privacy[2] he must not intrude upon.

The fisherlad turned to walk back to his small, empty croft. The moon cast a new light on the rocks by his feet. The bareness of the rock was covered by a moss of velvet seal skins. The fisherlad picked one up, not knowing why. Perhaps as a keepsake of that special glimpsed moment? Perhaps because

---

[2]**privacy**   private space

his hand touched the most beautiful skin on the rocks and couldn't let it go . . . We don't know. He carried it home feeling guilty and full of treasure. He knew he was holding the seal skin that a selkie must have before she could return to the sea – and he knew all selkies must return to sea.

The fisherlad felt he must hide his treasure and guilt. He climbed an old ladder to the thatched roof of his home and pushed the skin deep into the straw that was his roof and shelter. Dispensed of his beautiful burden, the lad wearily went to bed and to sleep.

He was woken early the following morning to a crying and a knocking at his door. On opening the latch to a windy, sunny dawn, he was amazed to see the most beautiful, long-haired girl standing crying in front of him. The night hours of dreaming had been filled with this girl and others, dancing. Now he remembered his act of impulse the night before. He knew who this must be. And yes, through her sobs, here she was asking if the fisherlad had possibly seen her seal skin . . . the skin she must have to return to the sea and her family. He couldn't tell the truth. He couldn't let her go. He told her that she could stay with him and be his wife. He told her how he loved her and would look after her.

The poor selkie girl had no choice. She married the fisherlad and, as the years went by, had three children. Also, as the years went by, she grew fond of her husband and loved her children dearly. But she was never totally at peace with herself. Every full moon, she'd look out of the window and cry softly as she heard her selkie family singing nearby. She loved the sea and would, whenever she could, take her children down to swim and paddle in the shallow cold waters.

This was the life of the selkie girl and her fisherlad husband for seven years. Then one day the children found their mother's seal skin. It was a spring morning and they'd been playing outside, clambering on the old straw roof of their home hunting for birds' nests, counting eggs. A small arm and hand felt down a hole in the straw expecting to feel warm, smooth, new-laid eggs. Instead a strange, wet, furry object was pulled out and wondered at. The children rushed to show their mother this unexpected find, not knowing that it belonged to her.

The mother felt her heart break in two when she saw her children appearing with the skin. She realized her husband must have hidden this from her. Compulsion[3] drew her to snatch this true part of herself from her children and run down to the rocks. She pulled on her old, wet skin and dived into the deep cold waters that were her home. Nature called her back to join her selkie family.

Further reading

You can find a vast collection of myths and folk tales, including transformation myths and versions of this tale at:
http://www.pitt.edu/~dash/folktexts.html

For other short stories from Scotland, see *The Oxford Book of Scottish Short Stories* (edited by Douglas Dunn; Oxford University Press, 2001).

---

[3]**compulsion**   the condition of having to do something

Out of Bounds (South Africa)

by Beverley Naidoo

> Apartheid forced the people of South Africa to live apart as Blacks,
> Whites, Indians and 'Coloureds' for nearly fifty years. Beverley
> Naidoo's *Out of Bounds* is an anthology of stories about the choices
> made by young people in a country that was full of injustice. These
> stories, including the title story, show that, despite the conflict,
> some young people stood up for what they believed to be moral and
> right.

Out of bounds. That's what his parents said as soon as the squatters[1] took over the land below their house. Rohan's dad added another metre of thick concrete bricks to their garden wall and topped it with curling barbed wire. He certainly wasn't going to wait for the first break-in and be sorry later. They lived on the ridge of a steep hill with the garden sloping down. Despite the high wall, from his bedroom upstairs, Rohan could see over the spiked-wire circles down to the place where he and his friends used to play. The wild fig trees under which they had made their hideouts were still there. They had spent hours dragging planks, pipes, sheets of metal and plastic – whatever might be useful – up the hill from rubbish tipped in a ditch below. The first squatters pulled their hideouts apart and used the same old scraps again for their own constructions: Rohan could still see the 'ski-slope' – the red earth down which he and his friends had bumped and flown on a couple of old dustbin lids. The squatters used it as their road up the hill. Now it looked like a crimson scar cut between the shacks littering the hillside.

'There's only one good thing about this business,' Ma said after the back wall was completed. 'We won't have to wash that disgusting red dust out of your clothes any more!'

---

[1]**squatters**   people who settle in a property to which they have no legal right

Rohan said nothing. How could he explain what he had lost?

At first, some of the squatter women and children came up to the houses with buckets asking for water. For a couple of weeks his mother opened the gate after checking that no men were hanging around in the background. She allowed the women to fill their buckets at the outside tap. Most of her neighbours found themselves doing the same. Torrential rains and floods had ushered in the new millennium by sweeping away homes, animals and people in the north of the country. The television was awash with pictures of homeless families and efforts to help them. No one knew from where exactly the squatters had come. But, as Ma said, how could you refuse a woman or child some water?

It wasn't long before all that changed. The first complaint of clothes disappearing off the washing line came from their new neighbours. The first African family, in fact, to move in among the Indians on Mount View. No one had actually seen anyone but everyone was suspicious including the neighbour, Mrs Zuma.

'You can't really trust these people, you know,' Mrs Zuma tutted when she came to ask if Ma had seen anyone hanging around. However, it was when thieves broke into old Mrs Pillay's house, grabbed the gold thali[2] from around her neck and left her with a heart attack, that views hardened. Young men could be seen hanging around the shacks. Were some of them not part of the same gang? Mrs Pillay's son demanded the police search through the settlement immediately. But the police argued they would need more evidence and that the thieves could have come from anywhere.

A new nervousness now gripped the house-owners on top of the hill. Every report of theft, break-in or car hijacking, any-where in the country, led to another conversation about the

---

[2]**thali**   the chain and pendant tied by the groom around the bride's neck in a Hindu wedding

squatters on the other side of their garden walls. At night Rohan peered through the bars of his window before going to sleep. Flickering lights from candles and lamps were the only sign that people were living out there in the thick darkness. In the daytime, when Ma heard the bell and saw that it was a woman or child with a bucket, she no longer answered the call. All the neighbours were agreed. Why should private house-owners be expected to provide water for these people? That was the Council's job. If the squatters were refused water, then per-haps they would find somewhere else to put up their shacks. A more suitable place. Or even, go back to where they came from.

The squatters did not go away. No one knew from where they managed to get their water or how far they had to walk. On the way to school, Rohan and his dad drove past women walking with buckets on their heads.

'These people are tough as ticks![3] You let them settle and it's impossible to get them out,' complained Dad. 'Next thing they'll be wanting our electricity.'

But Rohan wasn't really listening. He was scanning the line of African children who straggled behind the women and who wore the black and white uniform of Mount View Primary, his old school. He had been a pupil there until his parents had moved him to his private school in Durban with its smaller classes, cricket pitch and its own rugby ground. Most of the African children at Mount View had mothers who cleaned, washed and ironed for the families on top of the hill. But since the new year they had been joined by the squatter children and each week the line grew longer.

The queue of traffic at the crossroads slowed them down, giving Rohan more time to find the 'wire car' boy. He was looking for a boy who always steered a wire car in front of him with a long handle. He was about his own age – twelve or thirteen perhaps – and very thin and wiry himself. What

---

[3]**ticks** small bloodsucking parasites

interested Rohan was that the boy never had the same car for more than two or three days. Nor had he ever seen so many elaborate designs simply made out of wire, each suggesting a different make of car. They were much more complicated than the little wire toys in the African Crafts shop at the Mall.

'Hey, cool!' Rohan whistled. 'See that, Dad?' The boy must have heard because he glanced towards them. His gaze slid across the silver bonnet of their car towards the boot but didn't rise up to look at Rohan directly.

'It's a Merc – like ours, Dad! What a beaut! Do you think – '

'*Don't* think about it, son! You want us to stop and ask how much he wants, don't you?'

Rohan half-frowned, half-smiled. How easily his father knew him!

'No way! If we start buying from these people, we'll be encouraging them! That's not the message we want them to get now, is it?'

Rohan was quiet. He couldn't argue with his dad's logic. If the squatters moved away, he and his friends could get their territory back again.

Rohan returned home early from school. A precious half-day. In the past he would have spent it in his hideout. Instead he flicked on the television. News. As his finger hovered over the button to switch channels, the whirr of a helicopter invaded the living room.

'Hey, Ma! Look at this!'

Ma appeared from the kitchen, her hands cupped, white and dusty with flour. On the screen, a tight human knot swung at the end of a rope above a valley swirling with muddy water.

A South African Air Force rescue team today saved a baby from certain death just an hour after she was born in a tree. Her mother was perched in the tree over floodwaters that have devastated Mozambique. The mother and her baby daughter were among the lucky few. Many thousands of Mozambicans are still waiting to be lifted to safety from branches and rooftops. They have now been marooned for days by the rising water that has swallowed whole towns and villages.

'Those poor people! What a place to give birth!' Ma's floury hands almost looked ready to cradle a baby. Rohan was watching how the gale from the rotors forced the leaves and branches of the tree to open like a giant flower until the helicopter began to lift. Members of the mother's family still clung desperately to the main trunk. Rohan saw both fear and determination in their eyes. He and Ma listened to the weather report that followed. Although Cyclone Eline was over, Cyclone Gloria was now whipping up storms across the Indian Ocean and heading towards Mozambique. Where would it go next? Durban was only down the coast. Rohan had seen a programme about a sect who believed the new millennium would mark the end of the world. They were convinced that the floods were a sign that The End was beginning.

'What if the cyclone comes here, Ma?'

'No, we'll be all right son. But that lot out there will get it. The government really should do something.' Ma nodded in the direction of the squatters.

'Now, let me finish these *rotis*[4] for your sister!'

Ma returned to her bread-making. When she had finished, she wanted Rohan to come with her to his married sister's house. He pleaded to stay behind.

'I've got homework to do Ma! I'll be fine.'

'You won't answer the door unless it's someone we know, will you?'

'No Ma!' he chanted. Ma said the same thing every time.

Alone in the house, Rohan daydreamed at his desk. He was close enough to the window to see down the hill. What if there was so much rain that a river formed along the road below! As the water rose, people would have to abandon their shacks to climb higher up. They would be trapped between the flood below and the torrents above. In assembly they had heard the story of Noah building the Ark. Perhaps it wasn't just a story

---

[4]***rotis*** flat unleavened bread eaten in India

after all. Perhaps the people had tried to cling on to the tops of trees as tightly as those they had seen on television.

Tough as ticks.

The phrase popped into his mind. Wasn't that what his dad had said about the squatters? Yet the one sure way to get rid of ticks was to cover them in liquid paraffin. Drown them. A terrible thought. He should push it right away.

Rohan was about to stretch out for his maths book when a figure caught his eye on the old ski-slope. It was the thin wiry boy but he wasn't pushing a car this time. He was carrying two large buckets, one on his head, the other by his side. He descended briskly down the slope and turned along the road in the opposite direction to that taken by the women who carried buckets on their heads. Rohan followed the figure until he went out of sight, then forced himself to open his book.

The bell rang just as he was getting interested in the first question. Nuisance! He hurried to the landing. If someone was standing right in front of the gate, it was possible to see who it was from the window above the stairs. He stood back, careful not to be seen himself. It was the same boy, an empty container on the ground each side of him! Didn't he know not to come to the house up here? But he was only a child and it looked as if he just wanted some water. It would be different if it were an adult or a complete stranger. Rohan's daydream also made him feel a little guilty. He could see the boy look anxiously through the bars, his hand raised as if wondering whether to ring the bell again. Usually when the boy was pushing his wire car on the way to school, he appeared relaxed and calm.

By the time the bell rang a second time, Rohan had decided. He hurried downstairs but slowed himself as he walked outside towards the gate.

'What do you want?' Rohan tried not to show that he recognized the boy.

'I need water for my mother. Please.' The boy held his palms out in front of him as if asking for a favour. 'My mother – she's having a baby – it's bad – there's no more water. Please.'

This was an emergency. Not on television but right in front of him. Still Rohan hesitated. His parents would be extremely cross that he had put himself in this situation by coming to talk to the boy. Weren't there stories of adults who used children as decoys to get people to open their gates so they could storm in? He should have stayed inside. Should he tell the boy to go next door where there would at least be an adult? But the boy had chosen to come to here. Perhaps he had seen Rohan watching him from the car and knew this was his house.

'We stay there.' The boy pointed in the direction of the squatter camp. 'I go to school there.' He pointed in the direction of Mount View Primary. He was trying to reassure Rohan that it would be OK to open the gate. He was still in his school uniform but wore a pair of dirty-blue rubber sandals. His legs were as thin as sticks.

'Isn't there a doctor with your mother?' It was such a silly question that as soon as it was out, Rohan wished he could take it back. If they could afford a doctor, they wouldn't be squatters on a bare hillside. The boy shook his head vigorously. If he thought it was stupid, he didn't let it show on his troubled face.

'Wait there!' Rohan returned to the house. The button for the electric gate was inside the front door.

The boy waited while the wrought-iron bars slowly rolled back.

'OK. Bring your buckets over here.' Rohan pointed to the outside tap. The buckets clanked against each other as the boy jogged towards him.

'Thank you,' he said quietly.

The unexpected softness in his voice had a strange effect on Rohan. It sounded so different from his own bossy tone. Suddenly he felt a little ashamed. This was the same boy whose wire cars he admired! If he were still at Mount View Primary they would probably be in the same class. They might even have been friends and he would be learning how to make wire cars himself. Why had he spoken so arrogantly? It was really only a small favour that was being asked for. The water in the bucket gurgling and churning reminded Rohan of the water swirling beneath the Mozambican woman with her baby. *Her* rescuer had been taking a really big risk but hadn't looked big-headed. He had just got on with the job.

When both buckets were full, the boy stooped to lift one on to his head. Rohan saw his face and neck muscles strain under the weight. How would he manage to keep it balanced and carry the other bucket too?

'Wait! I'll give you a hand.' Rohan's offer was out before he had time to think it through properly. If the boy was surprised, he didn't show it. All his energy seemed to be focused on his task. Rohan dashed into the kitchen to grab the spare set of keys. Ma would be away for another hour at least. He would be back soon and she need never know. It was only after the gate clicked behind them, that Rohan remembered the neighbours. If anyone saw him, they were bound to ask Ma what he was doing with a boy from the squatter camp. He crossed the fingers of one hand.

At first Rohan said nothing. Sharing the weight of the bucket, he could feel the strain all the way up from his fingers to his left shoulder. When they reached the corner and set off down the hill, the bucket seemed to propel them forward. It was an effort to keep a steady pace. Rohan glanced at the container on the boy's head, marvelling at how he kept it balanced. He caught the boy's eye.

'How do you do that? You haven't spilt a drop!'

The boy gave a glimmer of a smile.

'You learn.'

Rohan liked the simple reply. He should ask the boy about the cars. This was his chance, before they turned into the noisy main road and reached the squatter camp.

'I've seen you with wire cars. Do you make them yourself?'

'Yes – and my brother.'

'You make them together? Do you keep them all?'

'My brother – he sells them at the beach.' The boy waved his free hand in the direction of the sea. 'The tourists – they like them.'

'Your cars are better than any I've seen in the shops! Do you get lots of money for them?'

'Mmhh!' The boy made a sound something between a laugh and a snort. Rohan realized that he had asked another brainless question. Would they be staying in a shack if they got lots of money? Rohan had often seen his own father bargaining to get something cheaper from a street hawker. He tried to cover his mistake.

'There's a shop in the Mall where they sell wire cars. They charge a lot and yours are a hundred times better!'

'We can't go there. The guards – they don't let us in.'

Rohan knew the security guards at the entrance to the Mall. Some of them even greeted his parents with a little salute. Rohan had seen poor children hanging around outside. They offered to push your trolley, to clean your car – anything for a few cents. Sometimes Ma gave an orange or an apple from her shopping bag to a child. Other times she would just say 'No thank you' and wave a child away. Ma never gave money. She said they might spend it on drugs. Rohan had never thought what it would be like to be chased away. How did the guards decide who could enter? How could the boy and his brother go and show the lady in the African Crafts shop his cars if they weren't allowed in?

Rohan was quiet as they reached the main road and turned towards the squatter camp. The noise of vehicles roaring past was deafening. He never normally walked down here. Not by himself nor with anyone else. His family went everywhere by car. With all the locks down, of course. The only people who walked were poor people. His eyes were drawn to a group of young men walking towards them. They were still some distance away but already Rohan began to feel uneasy. They were coming from the crossroads that his dad always approached on full alert. Rohan knew how his father jumped the red lights when the road was clear, especially at night. Everyone had heard stories of gangs who hijacked cars waiting for the lights to change.

The handle had begun to feel like it was cutting into his fingers. The boy must have sensed something because he signalled to Rohan to lower the bucket. For a few seconds they each stretched their fingers.

'It's too far? You want to go?' The boy was giving him a chance to change his mind. To leave and go back home. He had already helped carry the water more than half the way. He could make an excuse about the time. But the thought of running back to the house along the road on his own now worried him.

'No, it's fine. Let's go.' Rohan heard a strange brightness in his own voice. He curled his fingers around the handle again.

As they drew nearer the men, Rohan felt their gaze on him and suddenly his head was spinning with questions. Why on earth had he offered to help carry the water? What did he think he was doing coming down here? And he hadn't even yet entered the camp itself!

'We go here.' The boy's voice steadied him a little.

Rohan turned and stared up at his old ski-slope. He felt the force of the young men's eyes on his back as he and the boy began to ascend the rough track. Someone behind called out something in Zulu and, without turning, the boy shouted back. The words flew so quickly into one another that Rohan didn't pick up any even though he was learning Zulu in school. They must be talking about him but he was too embarrassed – and frightened – to ask. He could feel his heart pumping faster and told himself it was because of the stiff climb. He needed to concentrate where he put each foot. The track was full of holes and small stones. A quick glance over his shoulder revealed that the young men had also entered the squatter camp but seemed to be heading for a shack with a roof covered in old tyres on the lower slope. A couple of them were still watching. He must just look ahead and control his fear. As long as he was with the boy, he was safe, surely?

A bunch of small children appeared from nowhere, giggling and staring. He couldn't follow their chatter but heard the word '*iNdiya!*' The boy ignored them until a couple of children started darting back and forth in front of them sweeping up the red dust with their feet.

'*Hambani!*' Rohan could hear the boy's irritation as he waved them away. But the darting and dancing continued just out of reach.

'*Hambani-bo!*' This time the boy's voice deepened to a threat and the cluster of children pulled aside with one or two mischievous grins. Beads of sweat had begun trickling down the boy's face. With his own skin prickling with sticky heat, Rohan wondered at the wiry strength of the boy whose back, head and bucket were still perfectly upright as they mounted the hill.

'It's that one – we stay there.' The boy, at last, pointed to a structure of corrugated iron, wood and black plastic a little further up. It was not far from the old fig trees. For a moment Rohan thought he would say something about his hideout which the first squatters had pulled down. But he stopped himself. Maybe the boy had even been one of them!

As they drew nearer, they heard a woman moaning and a couple of other women's voices that sounded as if they were comforting her. The boy lowered the bucket swiftly from his head and pushed aside a plywood sheet, the door to his home. Rohan wasn't sure what to do. He knew he couldn't follow. The sounds from within scared him. The moans were rapid and painful. He remembered a picture in a book at school that had showed the head of a baby popping out between its mother's legs. There had been an argument among his friends about how such a big head could possibly fit through a small hole. From what he could hear now, it must hurt terribly. Rohan folded his arms tightly, trying not to show how awkward he felt. The little children were still watching but keeping their distance. They could probably also hear the cries. It would be hard to keep anything private here. The only other people near by were two grey-haired men sitting on boxes a little lower down the hill. One of them was bent over an old-fashioned sewing machine placed on a metal drum, a makeshift table. Normally Rohan would have been very curious to see what he was stitching but now he was just grateful that both men were engrossed in talking and didn't seem interested in him.

He turned to look up the hill – towards his house and the others at the top protected by their walls with wires, spikes and broken bottles. When he had hidden in his hideout down here, he had always loved the feeling of being safe yet almost in his own separate little country. But that had been a game and he could just hop over the wall to return to the other side, Surrounded now by homes made out of scraps and other people's leftovers, this place seemed a complete world away from the houses on the hill. In fact, how was he going to get home? If he didn't leave soon, Ma would be back before him. Would the boy at least take him part of the way through the squatter camp? He needed him to come outside so that he could ask him.

'What do you want here?'

Rohan spun around. A man with half-closed eyes and his head tilted to one side stood with his hands on his hips, surveying Rohan from head to foot. His gaze lingered for a moment on Rohan's watch.

'I–I brought water with . . . with . . .' Rohan stammered. He hadn't asked the boy his name! Panic-stricken, he pointed to the door of the shack. The man stepped forward and Rohan stumbled back against the wall of corrugated iron. The clattering brought the boy to the door. The man immediately switched into loud, fast Zulu. The boy spoke quietly at first but when the man's voice didn't calm down, the boy's began to rise too. Even when he pointed to the bucket and Rohan, the man's face remained scornful. Rohan was fully expecting to be grabbed when a sharp baby's cry interrupted the argument. The boy's face lit up and the man suddenly fell silent. Rohan's heart thumped wildly as the man's eyes mocked him before he turned and walked away.

Rohan folded his arms tightly, trying not to shake. Before he could say anything, a lady appeared behind the boy, placing a hand on his shoulder.

'You have a little sister!' She smiled at the boy and then at Rohan. She looked friendly but tired. Her cheeks shone as if she too had been perspiring. It was obviously hard work helping to deliver a baby.

'Tell your mother thank you for the water. You really helped us today.'

Rohan managed to smile back.

'It's OK.' His voice came out strangely small.

'Solani will take you back now – before it gets dark.'

Rohan felt a weight lifting. He did not need to ask.

The sun was getting lower and made long rod-like shadows leap beside them as they scrambled down the slope. Knowing the boy's name made Rohan feel a little easier and he wondered why he hadn't asked him earlier. He told Solani his own and the next thing he was telling him about riding on dustbin lids down the ski-slope. Solani grinned.

'It's good! But this place – it's a road now. We can't do it. The people will be angry if we knock someone down.'

Rohan understood that. But what he didn't understand was why the man with scornful eyes had been so angry with him. And why had those other young men looked at him so suspiciously? He decided to ask Solani.

'They don't know you. Sometimes people come and attack us. So if a stranger comes, they must always check first.'

When they reached the road, neither spoke. The home-time traffic would have drowned their voices anyway. Rohan thought about what Solani had said about him being a stranger. Surely they knew that he was from one of the houses on top of the hill. The houses that also did not welcome strangers. Like the squatters.

They parted at the top of the hill. Rohan was anxious to reach the house before his mother returned and Solani was eager to see his baby sister. Opening the electronic gates, Rohan was relieved that his mother's car was neither in the yard nor the garage. He dashed upstairs to his room and peered out of the window over to the squatter camp. The evening was falling very rapidly. His mother would be home any minute – and his dad. Neither liked to drive in the dark if they could help it. Rohan fixed his eyes on the deep crimson scar, hoping to see Solani climbing the slope. How strange to think that he had been there himself less than half-an-hour ago. In that other world. Yes! There was Solani! A tiny wiry figure bounding up the hill. Not hampered this time with a container of water on his head. Rohan watched Solani weave through other figures travelling more slowly until three-quarters of the way up the hill, he darted off and disappeared into the darkening shadow that was his home.

Rohan surprised his parents by joining them for the eight o'clock news. The story about the rescue of mother and baby from the floods in Mozambique was repeated.

Sophia Pedro and her baby daughter Rositha were among the lucky few. Many thousands of Mozambicans are still waiting to be lifted to safety . . .

This time the reporter added their names. Rohan observed the mother more closely. Had she also cried and moaned like Solani's mother? With the roaring waters underneath, how many people had heard her?

'It's nice to see these South African soldiers doing some good,' said Ma when the news was finished. Rohan wished he could say what he too had done that afternoon. But he feared the storm that it would let loose and went upstairs to his bedroom. Before slipping between his sheets, he peered out once again through the bars at the hill swallowed up by the night. He thought he saw a light still flickering in Solani's home and wondered how many people were tucked inside the sheets of iron, plastic and wood. He prayed that Cyclone Gloria would keep well away.

Next morning, the glint of metal beside the gate caught his eye from the front door. His dad was reversing the car out of the garage. Rohan ran across the drive. There, just inside the gate, was a wire car. A small, perfect Merc! Who could it be from, except Solani? He must have slipped it through the bars of the gate in the early morning. Quickly Rohan pushed it behind a cluster of scarlet gladioli. If his parents saw it, they would want to know from where it had come. They would discover he had gone out of bounds . . . Well, so had Solani! Each of them had taken a risk. He needed time to think. In the meantime, the car would have to be his secret. Their secret. His and Solani's.

Further reading

If you liked this story, have a look at others in Beverley Naidoo's collection *Out of Bounds* (Heinemann Educational Publishers, 2003). You might also like some of her novels, which include *The Other Side of Truth* (HarperTrophy, 2003), about two children who arrive in England as refugees, and *No Turning Back* (HarperTrophy, 1999), about a boy in South Africa who escapes his violent stepfather to live on the streets.

Mr Naidoo's Hundredth Birthday
(South Africa)

by Norman Silver

Many children have good friendships with adults outside their family. In this story, a boy tells us of his friendship with one of his father's employees. But people are not always what they seem . . . and, like our narrator, we as readers find out some startling things about the people we are introduced to.

In my last year of school I had a Saturday morning job at Valhalla Furniture. I worked mainly in the lighting department, demonstrating various lamps and light fittings for customers. My head was so filled with details of watts and volts, I'm sure it would have shone in the dark like a chandelier.

Naturally, I didn't do this job out of my own choice – I had better things to do on a Saturday morning than bringing light into people's lives. But my dad insisted I did this work. And it was he also who was responsible for the lousy pay I received. But what could I do about it? He owned Valhalla Furniture.

Working on that job I got to know Boola quite well. But really I think you have to put yourself in someone else's skin before you can understand them properly, wouldn't you say? All the more so if their skin is a different colour to yours. At any rate, that's what my ma always says about the handicapped people she works with at the Woltemade Centre.

Old Boola had been a handyman at Valhalla Furniture for years; he was quite good with hammer and nails and a wood-saw. All furniture assembly and such things were left for Boola, though he actually fancied himself as a bit of a sweet-talking salesman, and was always trying to get a piece of the sales action. I think he reckoned he could talk a man with no wife into buying a double bed, but as far as I know the closest he ever came to that was talking some old sailor into buying a rocking chair to remind him of the ocean waves.

My ma always took time to talk to Boola, on her brief visits to Valhalla.

'How's Meena doing?' she would ask every time.

I suppose my ma was interested in Boola's daughter because of her work with handicapped people. From what I could gather, Meena was a bit retarded.

'She's okay, Missus, but she struggles with the children, you know.'

'Is it four children?'

'It's five now, Missus.'

'Ag, shame,' my ma would say. 'What about a husband for her?'

'No, Missus, the men just take advantage of her, but they don't want to marry someone like her, even though she's got a heart of gold, I tell you.'

'Can't you arrange a marriage for her?'

'I've tried, Missus, but the only man I could get had a messed-up face.'

'What do you mean?'

'He was in a car accident and his face is very bad. No woman can look at him.'

'Did Meena meet him?'

'Yes, Missus, she said he was a nice man, very kind, and she would marry him, but after he spoke to her, he said to me he didn't want to marry a halfwit person.'

'Ag shame,' my ma said.

Boola struggled hard to support Meena and the children. He lived with them in some little house in the back of Retreat. I suppose that's why he tried to get in on the sales action, to earn a bit of commission.

But it became harder and harder to sell anything at Valhalla Furniture. Even the real salesmen were having trouble.

It was all the fault of the Portuguese opposite. They started up the Discount Furniture Centre in the huge Newgate shopping precinct that got built across the road from Valhalla. And my dad had to watch for three years how those guys built up their business, while those guys watched him going down the drain. They were ruthless, and reclaimed furniture after the first lapse of payment. You could see their heavies going out in their brand new vans and returning with the almost new furniture. Whereas my dad did his debt-collecting mostly on his own. One Saturday morning he took me with him.

I sat in our trusty old van as he knocked on the front door of this tin-roofed house in Plumstead. A huge man with a red face came to the door and I heard my dad explaining the situation to him. But he couldn't have explained it too well, because the red-faced chap started gesticulating[1] with both his enormous hands.

'A man's got to eat!' he screamed.

I thought what a pity my dad disturbed him during his meal.

'You think all I've got to do is pay you for that shitty table you sold us? Come in and see it, man, it's falling to bits.'

I wasn't surprised: if one of those gesticulations made contact with that table during a meal, it wouldn't have stood a chance. Nor would my dad's face, if he argued much longer.

'I didn't want that table in the first place. It's your salesman who told me I need to eat on a dining table. There was nothing wrong with my old kitchen table. If you can't wait another month, you can take back your piece of shit and shove it up your Jew-arse.'

Well, of course, in the end my dad was persuaded by those eloquent words and gesticulations to take pity on the man, and I don't know if he ever got paid for that table.

Meanwhile the Portuguese got richer and richer, and even our longstanding customers started frequenting the Discount Centre opposite. My dad would surely have developed ulcers had he gone on watching such ruthless men thrive while his own business went to the dogs. But the bankruptcy came

---

[1]**gesticulating**   using gestures, especially in an animated or excited manner, with or instead of speech

quickly and was over and done in a jiffy, and soon after, my dad got the job at the Plaza cinema, and he's never looked back, because he's always loved films and knows who acts in every one and who wrote the music and who directed it and so on.

But when Valhalla started getting into its troubles, Boola was very anxious about losing his job.

'Who will look after my daughter and my grandchildren, Boss Kush?' he asked my dad.

My dad had no answer, because you tell me, who's going to employ a shabbily dressed sixty-three-year-old Indian whose sweet-talking mouth dribbles saliva every now and again?

The last straw at Valhalla was the burglary. There had been a spate of shop burglaries nearby that had my dad seriously worried, because he knew Valhalla didn't have the most modern security. In fact, it didn't have security at all, because what my dad had done was to lay these wires across all the shop windows himself, as if they were a proper burglar alarm system. But the wires all went to this phoney board of electrical apparatus that he found somewhere, and it wasn't plugged into anything! The pretence was completed by this metal sign which he managed to get hold of and which read 'THIS PROPERTY IS PROTECTED BY TRIDENT SECURITY SYSTEMS.'

This pretence had obviously worked for the seven years my dad owned Valhalla, because it had never been burgled. He also had a lot of faith in the fact that the police station was just down the road. But these particular burglars must have had no respect for the police being so nearby, and they also weren't fooled by the sign. They stole thousands of rands worth of goods, mostly small furniture items, light fittings and rugs – it must have been well planned – and what's more, they even stole the metal Trident Security Systems sign.

My dad lost a lot of money, because the insurance company wouldn't pay up once they discovered my dad's so-called security system. It was an awful morning, standing there in an half-empty shop, realizing that the end had come. And it was all the more awful knowing the Portuguese across the road were watching and gloating at your misfortune.

But Boola wasn't there to see the end.

It's funny, now I look back on all the time Boola worked for my dad, I would never have guessed that he was the sort of person to do what he did. Even though once or twice I spoke to him about his life.

I remember once old Boola asked me about the Woltemade Centre where my ma worked. I think maybe he secretly wanted to know if they could help his daughter Meena in any way. In passing, I told him that the centre was named after this bloke Wolraad Woltemade, who rode out into the raging waves to save the lives of sailors who were shipwrecked in Table Bay a long time ago. Time after time he rode out, returning with desperate sailors clinging to his horse. Until his horse tired, and both man and beast sank beneath the waves.

'That's a smart story, Master Basil,' he said. 'You will be a good journalist. Then you must tell a smart story about me, hey?'

'What must I tell?'

'You can tell that Boola got his Standard 8[2] and then he worked for twenty-five years for Mr Swersky selling bicycles, and eighteen years for Mr Leopold making picture frames, and then for your father another seven years in the furniture trade.'

'That's not enough for a story,' I said.

'Man, it was enough for a life. Why not for a story?'

'Didn't anything interesting ever happen to you?'

'Of course, what do you think I am? Now let me remember.'

But old Boola's memories weren't so good, I reckon, because the best he could come up with was something about marrying a no-good girl who ran off with a coloured man, leaving him with a simple-minded daughter.

'And I've got good Indian and Malay blood in me, not like that bleddy Hotnot she ran off with!'

---

[2]**Standard 8**   the most basic education level

But on that occasion I never guessed what Boola had done. Nor another time long ago, when I must have been about twelve or so, and Boola helped me with my school woodwork project.

I had decided to make a wooden jigsaw puzzle with this great picture I had – actually it was a poster – of surfriders. I stuck it on to some plywood with glue, then drew the outlines of all the pieces on the back. But my attempts at using the fretsaw were abysmal.

'You can't use such a blunt blade!' Boola told me, when I showed him my efforts. 'This blade is smooth as a baby's bum.'

It looked sharp enough to me, but he ran his leathery old thumb over the blade to prove the point.

So I went to the hardware shop and bought a new pack of blades.

'This is how you use a fretsaw,' Boola said. 'You keep the blade moving steady like this, see, and you keep the blade nice and upright.'

I tried, but still my pieces chipped as I turned the corner.

In the end Boola did half of the sawing, and I did the other half.

'Hey, that's fine handiwork, hey!'

The jigsaw was great. There were 200 pieces of complicated puzzle, which would give anybody a hard time. Old Forbesy liked my work and gave me a good mark. Much better than the mark I got for making my perspex matchbox holder the year before.

Yes, looking back, it is easy to see that even while Boola was helping me with that jigsaw, I had no idea of the person who was sitting there so kindly helping me.

I only found out when these two men turned up in the lighting department at Valhalla and asked to see Mr Gopal Naidoo.

'We're from the Municipality of Cape Town,' the one man said. He was dressed in a smart, charcoal pinstriped suit.

'No Mr Gopal Naidoo works here,' I said.

'Are you sure?' the other man chimed in. His suit was navy blue, and he was carrying a box wrapped in shiny gold paper. 'Where's the manager of this place?'

'My father's the manager,' I said. 'Come with me.'

As they walked behind me, Mr Charcoal whispered to Mr Navyblue.

'You see, I told you he couldn't be at this place. That woman was halfwitted, man. She didn't even know her own name.'

When we reached my dad's partitioned-off office, he told them that there was no Mr Gopal Naidoo in his employ. Only a Mr Boola Naidoo.

Mr Navyblue raised his eyebrows.

'Did he use to work in the Parks Department?' he asked.

'I doubt it,' my dad said. 'He's been a handyman for years. I don't think he knows the first thing about gardening.'

'He didn't work as a gardener,' Mr Navyblue explained. 'He worked as a cleaner.'

'We better have a word with this Boola Naidoo!' Mr Charcoal said.

Boola came into the office, smiling and showing his brown teeth.

'Are you Mr Boola Naidoo?' Mr Charcoal asked.

'That's me,' Boola said.

'Do you know a Mr Gopal Naidoo?' Mr Navyblue asked.

'Yes, sir, that's my father.'

'Excellent,' Mr Navyblue said. 'We have been trying to locate him. We've got an address in Retreat for him, but when we got there, this woman told us he wasn't there, and we should try Valhalla Furniture. Where exactly can we find him?'

'Why you want to see him?' Boola asked.

'We understand the old boy is 100 years old today,' Mr Charcoal explained, 'so we have come to give him this gift and a certificate signed by the Mayor of Cape Town himself.'

'Thank you,' Boola said. 'I will give it to him.'

'That's good of you, but we need to have a photograph of your father receiving the award.'

'My father is not well,' Boola said. 'He's very ill. He cannot have a photograph.'

'I'm sorry he's not well,' Mr Charcoal said. 'But where is he at the moment?'

Boola had the look on his face like he was trying to sell a double bed to a man with no wife.

'He's ... he's ... he's at my brother's house in Port Elizabeth.'

'So when he claims his pension every month,' Mr Charcoal said, 'why does he give the address in Retreat?'

'Because ... because ... ' Boola wasn't having any luck selling his double bed. 'Because he always lives in Retreat except now when he is so ill. I send the money to him in Port Elizabeth.'

Mr Charcoal turned again to Mr Navyblue.

'There's some fishy business going on over here, don't you think?'

'Ja, I smell a rat,' Mr Navyblue answered.

'Look here, Mr Naidoo, the Municipality has been paying out a pension to Mr Gopal Naidoo for thirty-five years and for thirty-five years he has put his thumbprint on our claim forms. According to our records, he is 100 years old today. So we've come to pay him the respects of the Municipality and to give him this nice box of gifts and a certificate, but if he's in Port Elizabeth, then you tell me, how has he been filling in his claim form?'

Poor old Boola didn't know what to say.

'It's a serious offence to forge[3] a pension claim,' Mr Navyblue said.

'But what about the thumbprint?' my father said. 'You can't forge a thumbprint.'

'I think we'll take another ride to Retreat,' Mr Charcoal said, 'and you can come with us, Mr Naidoo.'

Old Boola bowed his head pathetically, and went off with the two men.

'I can't leave the shop,' my dad said to me, 'but let's get hold of your mom.'

---

[3]**forge**   to imitate (e.g. handwriting or a signature)

He made a quick phone call and within ten minutes my ma had collected me and we were off to Retreat to see if Boola needed help.

Once we found the street, it was easy to see which was Boola's little house. It was the one with the shiny black Ford from the Municipality parked outside.

We knocked on the door and this short plump lady in a shabby, worn-out pink dress answered.

'Yes, Boola is here,' she said, in a sweet child's voice. 'But he is talking to someone.'

'We will also talk to him, Meena,' my ma said, taking her confidently by the arm and leading her indoors.

The house was so small, just a front room and two back rooms and a kitchen. Two barefoot children were sitting on the floor of the front room, their noses runny and their clothes ragged. On the wall behind the couch was a faded picture of an elephant with many arms. The settee itself was covered with a large cloth, that might once have been an old curtain. On it Boola was sitting. He was hardly able to greet my ma.

I could hear the voices of Mr Charcoal and Mr Navyblue coming from one of the back rooms.

Meena sat down next to Boola. My ma and me kept standing.

'Why are those men looking in the room, Boola?' Meena asked him.

'They're just looking for papers,' Boola said.

Suddenly, the two men emerged. Mr Charcoal was triumphantly holding up a jar in his hands, well away from his nose, which appeared to be suffering from the effects of a noxious[4] smell.

If they were surprised to see my ma and me in that house, they didn't show it. Mr Charcoal just held up the jar and I could see it contained liquid.

---

[4]**noxious**   extremely unpleasant

'I'd like you to meet what is left of the 100-year-old Mr Gopal Naidoo!' Mr Charcoal said, giving us a closer look at the jar.

I couldn't believe it.

There in the liquid was an ancient old thumb.

The thumb of Mr Gopal Naidoo, Boola's father, deceased twenty-something years ago.

My ma remained silent.

Boola held his head down. He knew he was in big trouble.

'This is a serious offence, Mr Naidoo,' Mr Navyblue said. 'You will be hearing from us and the police in due course.'

Mr Charcoal and Mr Navyblue strutted off, pleased with their day's work.

'What was in the bottle, Boola?' Meena asked.

'It was our life's savings,' Boola answered her gently, putting his arm around her.

Further reading

Norman Silver has written two books for teenagers: *No Tigers in Africa* (Puffin, 1994) and *Python Dance* (Faber & Faber, 1994). His poetry is also excellent – have a look for his collections *The Walkmen Have Landed* (Faber & Faber, 1994), *Words on a Faded T-shirt* (Faber & Faber, 1991) and *Choose Your Superhero* (Hodder Children's Books, 1998).

Three poems (Iraqi Kurdistan)
by Choman Hardi

> How important to you is a sense of belonging, whether to your home, your community or your culture? The poet Choman Hardi was born in Iraqi Kurdistan, but had to flee from there more than once because of attacks on Kurdish people in Iraq. Her first three books of poetry were written in Kurdish. Now, however, she lives in England, and these poems are from her first poetry collection written in English. When writers are forced to leave their homeland, they very often leave behind their readers and the vital tool of their trade, their language.

Life for Us

In Qala-Chwalan,
in a holiday cottage with a courtyard
and a large swimming pool –
we watched the men undress,
dive into the water, get out,
drink a glass of cold beer,
have a few spoons of beans and salad
then dive in again,
making enormous splashes as they swam.

And we, fully dressed in the hot summer afternoon,
could tuck up our dresses
and dangle our feet in the water.

My male cousins, as young as I was
kept arguing;
Being a boy is better than being a girl
and doesn't swimming prove this?

The liquid round my ankles seduced me.
Fully dressed, I jumped in the pool
and held on to the slippery bars.

I loved the gentle embrace of water,
reducing the warmth of the sun.
It must have felt the same inside my mother,
simple and relaxing.

I became braver, let go of the bar,
but the next moment I was drowning,
my colourful clothes holding me down.
For a slight second as I plummeted
I saw my clothes spreading out
like petals, opening up in all directions.

The Middle Way

He describes the house as a maze
which she imagines getting lost in.
The bedrooms distant from each other,
long corridors and four toilets.
'Space enough for privacy,' he says
and she imagines feeling lonely.

She describes her toilets for him:
'No comfy seats where you can sit and read.
They're on the ground
and you have to squat and push.'

He's seen some in old French houses,
and thought they were disgusting.
They disagree about hygiene –
for him it is bathing every morning,
for her it's washing your bottom after poo.

They disagree about touching.
'Men are not supposed to hug,' he says.
That's crazy, she thinks.

He was born into his own bedroom
prepared months in advance
while she slept in her parents' room
until she was eleven.
For their children they agree
to find the middle way.

My Children

I can hear them talking, my children
fluent English and broken Kurdish.

And whenever I disagree with them
they will comfort each other by saying:
Don't worry about mum, she's Kurdish.

Will I be the foreigner in my own home?

Further reading

If you enjoyed these poems you might like Benjamin Zephaniah's novel *Refugee Boy* (Bloomsbury, 2001), which is about a boy whose parents are from two different cultures. To save his life, he is taken by his father to England, and is left there as a refugee. You might also like to try Meera Syal's brilliant adult book *Anita and Me* (Flamingo, 2002) about an Indian girl growing up in England.

Robert and the Dog (Nigeria)

by Ken Saro-Wiwa

I'll tell you this, I may be dead but my ideas will not die.

Ken Saro-Wiwa, 1995

How many of us would be willing to devote much of our life to opposing injustice? Ken Saro-Wiwa was a Nigerian author and political activist whose activities against injustice in Nigeria led to his execution by the Nigerian government.

Saro-Wiwa's people, the Ogoni, live on land rich in oil reserves. Saro-Wiwa recognised that, whilst the oil companies and the government were making a profit from the oil industry of the area, the Ogoni farmers and their lands were suffering. Much of his writing focuses on the suffering of the poor but, because of its political overtones, it was suppressed by the Nigerian authorities. Saro-Wiwa's political activity was so effective that the oil companies pulled out of the area in 1993. Ultimately, this cost him his life.

This thought-provoking story focuses on the relationship between a British couple living in Nigeria, their dog and their manservant.

Robert's new employer was a young medical doctor just returned from abroad. He was cheerful, exuberant[1] and polite. It was obvious to Robert that he had not been in the country for a long time. Because he did not once lose his temper, he did not shout at Robert, he called him by his first name, and always asked him about his wife, children and other members of his family. Robert, accustomed to moving from household to household, thought he had at last found fulfilment. The more so as the young doctor appeared to be a bachelor.

Stewards,[2] including Robert, prefer to serve a bachelor. Because every bachelor is as wax in the hands of his steward.

---

[1]**exuberant**   enthusiastic
[2]**steward**   a person who runs someone else's household

The latter determines what is to be spent on grocery, how much food is to be served at meal times, what is to be done with the remnants of food. In short, he holds the bachelor's life in his hands. And that is tremendous power.

Robert quickly settled into his new situation and took full control of the house. Experience had taught him never to occupy the servants' quarters, which were attached to the main house. It made dismissals or the abandonment of a situation rather messy. So it was that Robert's family lived in the filth and quagmire[3] of Ajegunle, which the wags[4] termed 'The Jungle'. In his one-bedroom apartment in The Jungle, Robert was king. And he always repaired[5] there nightly to exercise his authority over his wife and six children. The experience he had gained in running his household helped him a great deal in organising the life of each new employer. Robert was particularly happy in his new situation because the young man was carefree and happy. There was, as has been said, no wife breathing down Robert's neck and limiting his abundant authority. There were no children whose nappies and numerous clothes had to be washed. He did not have to cook several meals a day. The young man ate but once a day, except for the cup of coffee and toast early in the morning.

Trouble began when the young man announced after six months that his wife was about to join him. Robert's face fell visibly at the announcement. But he did not worry very much at the expected curtailment of his wide powers. Who knew, the lady might not be an ogre after all.

Which is precisely what happened in the event. The lady was as young and cheerful as her husband. She, too, took an interest in Robert. She was European and excited about her first visit to Africa. She appeared pleased to have Robert's assistance. She spent the day asking Robert about African food, watching Robert at work in the kitchen and lending a helping

---

[3]**quagmire** boggy ground
[4]**wags** people with mischievous humour
[5]**repaired** returned

hand where possible. She made sure Robert stopped work early so that he could get home to his family, and she did not make a fuss if Robert turned up late some odd mornings. And she got Robert paid every fortnight. She even offered to go and visit his wife and family in The Jungle. Robert carefully and politely turned down her offer. He could not imagine her picking her neat way through the filth and squalor of The Jungle to the hovel which was his home. Maybe, he thought, if she once knew where he lived and sampled the mess that was his home, her regard for him would diminish and he might lose his job. Yet the young lady extended every consideration to him. Robert began to feel like a human being, and he felt extremely grateful to his new employers.

The only source of worry in the new situation was the dog. For the young lady had arrived with a dog, called Bingo. And Robert watched with absolute amazement and great incredulity as the lady spoke tenderly to the dog. She ensured that he was well fed with tinned food and milk and meat and bones. And she held the dog lovingly in her arms, brushed his hair and tended him carefully. The dog appeared as important to the lady as her husband and, indeed, Robert thought, in the order of things, the dog was more important than himself. Try as hard as he might, he could not dismiss from his mind the fact that the dog was doing better than himself. And he detested this state of affairs. He could understand a dog being invited to eat up an infant's faeces. He could understand a stray, mangy dog with flies around its ears being beaten and chased away from the dwellings of men. He could understand a dog wandering around rubbish heaps in search of sustenance. But a dog who slept on the settee, a dog who was fed tinned food on a plate, a dog who was brushed and cleaned, a dog who drank good tinned milk, was entirely beyond his comprehension. On one occasion, the lady took the dog to a doctor. And that was the straw that broke the camel's back.

All that day, Robert felt his stomach turn. And when he got home in the evening and saw his children, with distended stomachs, gambolling in the filth that simmered in a swollen stream at his door, and watched them hungrily swallow small balls of *eba*, he asked himself, 'Who born dog?' And all of a sudden he developed a pathological hatred for Bingo the dog, his master's dog. All night long, he saw in the eye of his mind the dog cuddled in the warmth of the settee, which he would have to clean and brush in the morning. And he asked himself again and again, 'Who born dog?'

The object of Robert's hatred was totally oblivious of the feelings that he bred in the cook-steward. He revelled in the love of his master and mistress. He ate his food with relish and wagged his tail in contented gratitude. He loved and served the lady, doing as he was bid. And he wagged his tail contentedly at Robert. He slept in the day and kept watch over his owners at night. But each wag of his tail was like so many pinpricks in the heart of Robert, who secretly vowed to 'show' the dog some day.

That day duly arrived and much sooner than Robert had expected. The young doctor announced to him that they would be going away on holiday for six weeks. He wanted Robert to take care of the house. As they would not be travelling with the dog, he would be most delighted if Robert would be kind enough to take care of Bingo. They were going to leave enough tinned food and milk for Bingo and some money so Robert could purchase bones to supplement his food. He hoped Robert did not mind.

Not in the least, Robert replied. But in his innermost heart, he knew he had found the opportunity he wanted.

After the departure of the couple, Robert, true to his training, obeyed his master's orders to the letter. On the first and second days. On the third day, watching the dog lap his milk from a plate, a voice spoke to Robert. 'Who born dog?' And, to this ponderous[6] question, Robert could find no other answer than 'Dog.' And the anger in him welled. He looked at the dog, and the dog looked at him, wagging his tail. 'Well may you wag your tail,' Robert thought, 'but I can tell you, I'm not going to waste my life taking care of you.'

---

[6]**ponderous**   slow and thoughtful

He gathered up all the tins of dog food, all the tins of milk, tethered the dog to the settee and walked off, out of the house and the job he had loved to do. He gave the milk and dog food to his children when he got home.

And the dog died.

Further reading

To find out more about Ken Saro-Wiwa's life, see the website in his memory: http://www.remembersarowiwa.com

Another story with a more uplifting portrayal of the relationship between humans and animals is *The Cry of the Wolf* by Melvin Burgess (Puffin, 1995).

In the Name of My Father (Nigeria)
by Ken Wiwa

'Following in your father's footsteps' seems a rather old-fashioned idea in modern society – in the past a son would often follow his father's career path, but now we have much more choice. Yet even today some people feel under some pressure to do what their relatives have done before them; others are proud to continue practices or traditions that have been part of their family history.

In this article, Ken Saro-Wiwa's son talks about his relationship with his father, how he felt when he heard of his father's death, and his mixed feelings about following in his father's footsteps. To find out more about Ken Saro-Wiwa before beginning this article, read the introduction to his story *Robert and the Dog* (page 35).

Ken Saro-Wiwa

Ken Wiwa

'Your dad's dead.' For most of my adult life I'd lived in dread of hearing those words. Even before he became a global icon[1] of social justice I was keenly aware that my father's death, whenever it came, would have a profound impact on my life. Years

---

[1] **icon** an important and long-lasting symbol

before they killed him I would imagine what it would be like to receive the news. I would rehearse scenarios[2] in my head; how would I feel, how would I react? I never imagined, not even in my wildest calculations, that my father's death would have such an impact well beyond my personal universe.

On the day they killed him I remember walking up a hilly street in Auckland. I was 25 years old and had flown to New Zealand to try to lobby the Commonwealth Heads of State to intervene on behalf of my father, who had been sentenced to death at the end of October. At the top of the street I turned to view the sunset. Looking out over the city centre below me and out into the harbour in the distance, I watched the sun sink into the sea, casting a pale orange glow against the sky. I remember the exact moment he died. I was sitting in a restaurant chatting and laughing with friends when I felt a brief palpitation[3] in my chest – it felt like a vital connection had been ruptured inside me and I just knew. It was midnight in Auckland and midday in Nigeria and my father had just been hanged; his broken body lay in a shallow sandpit in a hut at the condemned prisoners' block at Port Harcourt Prison.

His death on 10 November 1995 shook the world. John Major described the trial that sent him to the gallows as a 'fraudulent[4] trial, a bad verdict, an unjust sentence'. Nelson Mandela thundered that 'this heinous[5] act by the Nigerian authorities flies in the face of appeals by the world community for a stay of execution'.[6] Bill Clinton and the Queen added their voices to the worldwide condemnation, Nigeria was suspended from the Commonwealth, countries recalled their diplomats[7]

---

[2]**scenarios**   imagined series of events
[3]**palpitation**   violent or quick heartbeat
[4]**fraudulent**   dishonest
[5]**heinous**   hateful, abominable
[6]**stay of execution**   a legal order whereby an execution is prevented from going ahead immediately
[7]**diplomats**   people appointed by a government to carry out negotiations and oversee relationships with another country or countries

and there were calls for economic sanctions[8] and a boycott of Shell oil.

Sitting here in my father's old office in the busy commercial quarter of the old town of Port Harcourt on the southern coast of Nigeria is a poignant[9] place for me as I look back on his death. I've been travelling in and out of Nigeria since the end of military rule in 1999, dividing my time between my family in Canada and my father's business interests here, and earlier this year I took a decision to relocate my centre of gravity, moving my family back to England while I concentrated on running the business here . . .

Outside here the streets vibrate to the rhythms of a town that mocks its nickname as the garden city. Where this part of Port Harcourt was once the genteel colonial quarters with elegant mansions and their spacious verandahs, postmodern Africa is busy decolonising the city with a familiar pattern of snarling traffic jams, uncollected refuse and brash expressions of architectural confusion; the whole noise and colour of a city floating on a wave of oil money that creates islands of startling wealth in a sea of dehumanising poverty.

I remember how I would often find my father staring out of these windows. 'Look out there,' he would say gesturing with his chin. 'Out there are all the stories a writer needs.' He would stare in silence with a frown on his face as if he was contemplating some regret. Looking back, I think of him sitting there trying to come to terms with what must have seemed like the impossible burden of bringing those untold stories to the attention of the world.

Writing was my father's great love – I'm never sure how many books he actually produced but he once claimed 25 including poetry anthologies, plays, memoirs, collections of essays, short stories and at least two novels. No doubt he would have loved to have been remembered as a man of letters and he had already

---

[8]**economic sanctions**   restrictions on economic trading (buying or selling goods and services) imposed by one country on another, for political reasons

[9]**poignant**   emotionally distressing

arrogated[10] to himself the literary ambition of forging[11] the uncreated conscience of his people in his soul. In the end he never quite managed to publish that book but then the greatest story he ever told was to die for his people, and it took his death to realise his ambition of placing his people on the world map.

If you head north-east out of Port Harcourt and into the flat, gently sloping floodplains of the Niger River Delta you will likely arrive in my community. To foreign eyes Ogoni must look like any other rural community in sub-Saharan Africa. Off the main road that runs east–west right across the 404 square miles of Ogoni territory, the tarred roads eventually give way to dirt tracks of mud red earth that take you into the villages. You could travel around the 120 or so Ogoni villages and you might not see much evidence of the oil industry that has been at the core of this story but somewhere among the dense mangroves, the palm trees and the giant irokos[12] are the flowstations and pipelines that have pumped 900 million barrels of oil out of the area since the natural resource was discovered there in 1958.

All told, there were once over a hundred oil wells, a petrochemical complex, two oil refineries and a fertiliser plant in the region. An area which, as my father once wrote, should have been as rich as a small Gulf state stood as an example of how Africa's rich natural resources have impoverished its people and the land they live off.

Associated natural gas has been flared into the atmosphere for over 40 years in Nigeria – pumping noxious[13] fumes into the atmosphere. Nigeria alone accounts for 28 per cent of total gas flared in the world and the flared gas volume in Nigeria translates into the crude oil equivalent of 259,000 barrels per day.

Apart from the gas flares there are the oil spills, the matrix of pipelines that criss-cross Ogoni, sometimes over farmlands and often in close proximity to human habitation. The

---

[10]**arrogated**   assumed the rights to something
[11]**forging**   forming with real effort
[12]**irokos**   African trees from which hardwood is sourced
[13]**noxious**   harmful to health

pipelines had been laid without impact assessment studies,[14] without community consultation, and were often laid over appropriated farmland with little or minimal compensation. Few locals dared to question the oil industry because to do so was seen to challenge the national security of the country since the governments of Nigeria are dependent on oil revenues for foreign exchange. It takes a brave man to block the flow of oil.

Few dared to question the cosy relationship between the oil companies and Nigeria's ruling elites until my father spoke out. Born on 10 October 1941, he grew up in a traditional home in Ogoni. He saw the coming of the oil industry and as a 17-year-old began writing letters to newspapers questioning the benefits when oil was first discovered in Ogoni. For the next 30 years his commentaries on the oil nexus[15] escalated until he became best known in Nigeria for his trenchant criticisms of the industry.

By exposing the double standards of oil companies who preached sound ecological virtues in the north while singing from an entirely different songsheet in Nigeria, my father earned powerful enemies and became a marked man. Censored by editorial boards and denied a pulpit[16] in a country where poverty made books a luxury, my father decided to abandon his writing and took his words to the streets. In 1990 he was instrumental in forming Mosop (Movement for the Survival of the Ogoni People), a grassroots organisation to mobilise our community to speak out for their rights. So successful was Mosop in raising awareness among the community that, within three years of forming the organisation, an estimated 300,000 of our people spilled out onto the streets of Ogoni during a protest march.

My father later insisted that if he had died that day he would have died a happy man. Instead, from that day, he was a marked man. He was arrested or detained on four separate

---

[14]**impact assessment studies**   a process that predicts the environmental impact of human development activities and suggests ways of lessening that impact
[15]**oil nexus**   the central part played by oil in Nigeria
[16]**pulpit**   a place from which religious speakers deliver sermons and speeches

occasions until his final arrest on 21 May 1994 following a riot in Ogoni at which four prominent chiefs were murdered. My father and hundreds of Ogoni were held for nine months without charge and when he was finally charged to court he was accused of procuring[17] his supporters to murder the four chiefs.

When my father was finally brought before a civil disturbances tribunal the case had dubious[18] merit even within the provisions of the Nigerian law under which he was prosecuted. International and independent observers of the trial criticised the proceedings as unfair and premeditated to deliver a miscarriage of justice and the trial became an international cause celebre. The sentencing and execution of my father and eight Ogoni was the day my destiny was locked into a path that I had spent my entire adult life trying to resist.

Long before Ken Saro-Wiwa became a symbol of resistance for the Ogoni, Nigerians and social justice activists around the world, he was my father. As a child I had idolised Jeje, as I called him, but when he chose to send me to private schools in England, the cultural dislocation opened up a distance between us. Although my father always wanted the best education for his seven children, he had expected that we would return home to apply our expensively trained minds to the problems at home. It was a trajectory[19] that many Nigerians had followed, returning home to good jobs and a society that could offer a good life and a basic standard of living to exiles returning home loaded with degrees and doctorates. By the time I had sleepwalked through Tonbridge School and the University of London I had no real idea who I was, what I wanted to do with my life and where I wanted to apply that expensive education. My father was apoplectic[20] and exasperated that his eldest son and namesake showed little or no ambition of following in his footsteps.

---

[17]**procuring**   bringing about
[18]**dubious**   doubtful
[19]**trajectory**   the path of something moving through space
[20]**apoplectic**   furious

Whatever my misgivings about this country because of my father's murder, I knew deep down that I had no choice but to return; my father's multiple legacies, literary, business, personal and political are centred here. His life and death have anchored me to Nigeria and over the past five years of coming and going I have developed the same love–hate relationship with this country that my father had.

Life goes on but the pain never goes, especially as he remains a convicted murderer in Nigeria's statute books, despite UN resolutions to revisit the trial and the intense lobbying of the Nigerian government. The current administration is slowly coming to terms with Ken Saro-Wiwa. President Olusegun Obasanjo and the governor of my state, Dr Peter Odili, have been true to their word in allowing my family to retrieve my father's bones for a proper burial . . .

I often wonder what my own children will make of their grandfather and the name and history they carry. How will they interpret his story, my own, for their own future? Up until now I have tried to avoid speaking to them about my father for fear of traumatising[21] them. There are hardly any mementos or memorials to my father's struggle in my house but this year my children will, for the first time take part in some of those celebrations. My two boys, aged eight and five, are if nothing else, cut from the same cloth as their grandfather because they have inherited their grandfather's strong sense of right and wrong. I guess most children their age have a strong moral centre but I am conscious that they are already aware of their history. Inevitably they didn't need me to fill in the gaps in the family tree.

I am conscious that my relationship with my father, with their history and community, will have an impact on the direction of their lives. I am loath[22] to steer or direct them in any way for fear of repeating my father but my sense or at least my hope is that they will, like me, eventually find their own way and make

[21]**traumatising**   seriously upsetting
[22]**loath**   reluctant

an accommodation through his story. I feel that my job is to ensure that they learn the truth about my father, guide them and leave them with enough clues to give them a secure sense of the past so that they can shape their future.

Further reading

Another story in this collection that focuses on following in a father's footsteps is *Cut Me, and I Bleed Khaki* by Terence Blacker (page 73).

If you are interested in the life and writing of Ken Saro-Wiwa, you might like the anthology of poetry that was put together in his memory: *Dance the Guns to Silence* (Flipped Eye Publishing, 2005).

To find out more about political issues where corruption is part of the relationship between governments and big business at the expense of local people, visit the Survival International website at http://www.survival-international.org

A Place to Call Home (England)
by Simon Armitage

Many of the texts in this collection focus on the issues and identities of different countries around the world. Even within a country, however, different groups of people have their own distinct identities and cultures. *All Points North* (Viking, 1998), the book from which *A Place to Call Home* is taken, highlights the distinct identity of one such group – the people of the north of England – and also comments more generally on the common thoughts and concerns of English people at the very end of the 20th century.

Simon Armitage does not offer judgement or criticism of the people he describes, instead adopting an affectionate and wry tone. He does not ridicule, but the details he chooses to tell us about the lives he observes are often humorous.

Driving around looking for a house to buy, you stray over the top into Lancashire, and call in at a friend's farm in Strinesdale, only to find that it's been the site of a terrible tragedy. During last night's thunderstorms, forked lightning hit the paddock in front of the house, and the cow that was grazing there was killed. It lies in a big black heap by the gate, steaming in this morning's sun, at the end of a long muddy streak where Roy towed it back from the field with the JCB. The cow was in calf, and a bullock in the same field – last year's offspring – mopes and mooches at the top of the hill, refusing to come into the barn. Waiting for the knackers,[1] Roy tells you that for some reason cows are more susceptible to lightning strikes than horses, which surprises you, not just because horses are taller and therefore a more obvious target, but because they wear metal shoes. You also wonder how much the statistics for this kind of thing have been skewed[2] by foul play, remembering what a vet

---

[1] **knacker**   a person who buys old or sick animals and slaughters them to sell the meat or hide

[2] **skewed**   distorted or biased

once told you. During his career he said he'd been called to umpteen farms where cows had been 'struck by lightning', only to find a diseased corpse at the end of a pair of tyre tracks, dumped beneath a burnt tree with the smell of petrol still in the air. Cows killed by acts of God qualify for insurance money, and can also be sold to the abattoir[3] for meatstuffs.

Not that foul play is a possibility in this case. Roy retired from a job in the city last year, and all the animals on the farm are pets really, with names and collars around their necks. You can see that he's genuinely upset and anxious about the dead cow, but at the same time there's a kind of excitement in his face, as if something truly agricultural has happened, making him a proper farmer for the first time, not just a retired businessman with a smallholding[4] on the outskirts of Oldham. You drive back over the border, across the motorway bridge at Scammonden, thinking about Roy in the JCB, scooping the cow up in the bucket and tipping its great stiffening mass into the knacker's van, watching it trundle down the lane.

The next house on the list is in a quiet wooded valley in Calderdale not far from the M62 and on the right side of the county boundary. The property is one-third of an old mill-owner's house, miles too big and miles too expensive, but the estate agent was adamant[5] that you looked at it, and you park at the top of the drive and walk down through a walled garden, between two lines of monkey puzzle trees. The couple who own it are in their mid thirties with a two-year-old girl and another on the way. 'We're moving nearer town,' says Morag, in a Scottish accent infiltrated by Yorkshire vowels. 'Jim gets called into work so much, it's silly not to be nearer.'

Visits to houses nearly always start with the vendors[6] supplying this kind of information, giving a legitimate reason for

---

[3]**abattoir**   slaughterhouse
[4]**smallholding**   a small farm, usually under 50 acres
[5]**adamant**   insistent
[6]**vendors**   sellers

leaving, rather than letting on about the poltergeist that refuses to budge despite exorcisms from the Bishop of Wakefield, or plans that were recently passed for the siting of a glue factory and tannery in the next field. Another experience common to house-hunters in Calderdale is to find that the property usually hosts an electricity pylon in the back garden, and that a thousand-megavolt power line passes within spitting distance of the front bedroom. Rather than drive around the area looking for For Sale boards, buyers are better advised to follow the miles of thick grey cables, or look for the pylons that hold them, like a tug-of-war team holding their ground against the next village. All the decent houses are directly beneath.

At Valley Ford House there is no pylon, but there must be a power station nearby to supply all the various gadgets and gizmos in the place, beginning with the music system. Jim slides back the cover of a cabinet in the living-room, revealing something like the instrument panel of the space shuttle, and talks you through the various knobs and dials, assuring you of its value and reminding you that they won't be taking it with them when they move. In every room, Morag reels off the thickness of the carpet and the depth of the alcoves. Then Jim steps in with a handset, points it at a flashing panel somewhere in the ceiling, and the sound of Luther Vandross on CD or Danny Baker on Radio 1 or Richard and Judy on daytime television rises and falls as he runs his thumb up and down the volume control.

'We thought the wardrobes were MFI, so we were going to chuck them,' says Morag in the bedroom, 'but it turned out they're Strachan, so we left them in, obviously.' She carries on into the *en suite* bathroom, pointing out the shower unit with the wooden seat, the heated towel rail, the oval jacuzzi and the low-flush toilet and bidet, until she reaches the window at the far end. 'And this is the window,' she says, then nods at Jim, who draws his handset from its holster, and Elton John ricochets[7] between the hand-painted tiles and the full-length mirrors.

---

[7]**ricochets**   rebounds

Downstairs, you're led into a drawing-room with a red carpet, red walls and a red ceiling, reminiscent of the surgeon's room on HMS *Victory*, painted that colour to disguise the blood. 'We call it the red room. Jim, pull the shutters to show how dark it is.' Jim closes the wooden shutters on the two windows, and we stand there in the pitch black, with only the pulsing of a tiny red light in the sensor panel above us, like a distant star. In the kitchen, there's an ornate wood-burning stove, like a green postbox, in the fireplace. 'Does it draw?' you ask her.

'Excuse me?'

'Does it draw the smoke and keep the fire going?'

'Oh', she says, 'actually we've never had it lit.'

In every room there's a mobile phone charging in a socket, and so many pieces of communication equipment such as faxes and modems and answerphones that you wonder why Jim has to go to work at all, let alone move closer to it. The finale of the tour takes place in a cupboard under the stairs, where Jim demonstrates a telephone exchange that could probably facilitate the Yorkshire Water complaints department, with lines to spare. At one moment, he turns to you and says, 'But the great beauty of this system is that you can block your guests from making international phone calls.' You picture your mum and dad, staying over one night, surreptitiously lifting the receiver at three in the morning, foiled in their efforts to get through to Montevideo or Karachi. You think of the plastic telephone/ address book you once bought them with the sliding catch and the pop-up cover, wondering if it actually contains a single number for someone in another country.

House-hunting in Farnley Tyas, one of Huddersfield's most sought-after outlying villages, and probably most burgled. Sandra, going out to Durban with her husband's job, shows you the fitted kitchen. 'This is the griddle, this is the hob, this is the fan-assisted oven – you should knock half an hour off your meat with that – and this is the turbo grill, for barbecue chicken. Have you tried barbecue chicken? It's very tasty.' The dining table is a slab of granite, part of the bedrock that the house must have been built around. Framed in the bathroom window, Emley Moor Mast, like the after-burn of a rocket disappearing into the clouds. In the children's bedroom, she's stuck luminous stars to the walls and ceiling in their correct celestial positions. 'When I'm stressed, I lie down in here, turn out the lights and pretend I'm outside.' She flops back on to the bed and laughs, kicks her legs in the air, with the Mr Moon and Mr Sun wall-lamps beaming at each side of her, under the constellation of Cygnus the Swan.

House-hunting in Luddenden Foot, or Clubbenden Foot, as it's known. You follow directions down an unmade road to the cottage, where there are already five or six cars parked alongside the garden fence. Inside, the estate agent's representative is showing a handful of prospective buyers around the house, but as soon as you step over the threshold you become one of half a dozen disinterested parties. Clothes are strewn on the floor of every room, knickers and socks are erupting from every drawer, boxes of batteries and videos are tipped out on to a table, washing-up festers in the sink, children's toys – most of them broken – are herded into corners, and spores of talcum powder are still filtering through the air. It looks and feels as if some unmentionable practice had been going on over a number of years, which came to an end this morning, just an hour or so before the police arrived and turned the place over. A woman in a blue dress comes out of a bedroom with a handkerchief over her mouth. People pass each other at the head of the stairs and grimace, silently. Nobody dares look in the bathroom. Through the window, the 'rock-pool' in the garden is a puddle of piss-coloured water on a sheet of tarpaulin, covering who knows what. Everywhere the smell of damp, like a dungeon.

You go outside for some fresh air and see that the gable-end of the house is built into a banking, which then rises steeply above the roof. More than that, it's as if the house is retaining the hillside, shouldering the moor, shoring up the whole of the Pennines which are ready now to slump into the valley bottom, roll over like an animal on to its back, burying the abandoned cottage and all of the evidence.

House-hunting in Holmfirth. You're shown around a three-storey Victorian house by Mrs Micklethwaite, who finally leads you up to the attic to point out the two rooms in the roof space. She walks to the far wall, towards a tiny door with a wooden handle, saying, 'And this is just a cubby-hole, really.' Inside the room, which is about six-feet square and without a window, three sons and their father are huddled around a computer screen, playing a video game. The father, his eyes fixed to the screen, raises the back of his hand towards you, which you take to be the 'Hello' of a man who doesn't want to be disturbed. Thinking about it afterwards, you can see that it also meant 'silence', and 'halt', and 'goodbye'.

Further reading

If you enjoyed Simon Armitage's non-fiction, you might like to read some of his poetry. You could begin with Kid (Faber & Faber, 2002) or Zoom! (Bloodaxe Books, 1989).

Activities

The Seal Wife

Before you read

1   Look carefully at the image on page 4 and write down your answers to questions a to d.

   a   What five adjectives would you use to describe this setting?

   b   Can you find three small details that you think other people might not notice?

   c   What wildlife can you see?

   d   What stories and mythological characters do you know of that are associated with the sea?

   Discuss your ideas with the rest of your class.

What's it about?

Read the story and write down your answers to questions 2 and 3.

2   Explain in a sentence why the selkies dance on the night of the full moon.

3   People often use myths in order to make sense of the natural world and what happens there. The opening section of the story (paragraphs one to four) firmly establishes the setting of the story in the Scottish islands. List the elements of the natural world in Scotland to which the opening of this story refers.

Thinking about the text

4   How does the final line of the story relate to the language of the opening of this tale? Does it help to explain the girl's actions in leaving her family? Discuss your ideas with the rest of your class.

5   Think carefully about the motivation for the boy's actions and why he never told his wife the truth. Consider the girl's actions and why she finally left her family at the end of the story. Write down two questions that you would like to ask each character about their behaviour and motivation. In a small group, hot-seat each of these characters and ask your questions.

Out of Bounds

Before you read

1   Discuss questions a to c in a small group.
    a   What does the word 'prejudice' mean?
    b   Have your ever experienced prejudice?
    c   Have you ever judged someone before you got to know them, and then changed your mind about them later?

What's it about?

Read the story and write down your answers to questions 2 to 4.

2   The title of the story suggests restrictions and lack of freedom. How is this emphasised in the first paragraph, in which the author describes the setting? Pick two quotations to support your answer.

3   'Rohan half-frowned, half-smiled' (page 10). Write a sentence or two explaining the reasons for Rohan's expression.

4   Select three examples of language that convey Rohan's fear as he enters the camp on pages 15–16. Draw a two-column table with the headings 'The examples of words/groups of words' and 'How they create a sense of fear and tension'. Then complete the table to show how the writer builds up tension in the story.

Thinking about the text

5   This story addresses many issues linked both to South African politics and to personal relationships. Think carefully about what you think is the most crucial issue of this story for you. Then think of a new title for this story and write a paragraph explaining the reasons for your choice. Discuss your choice with the rest of your class.

6   Why is the news item on Mozambique crucial to the structure of this story? Working with a partner, scan the story to identify where the news item is mentioned. Then discuss why it is so important in this story.

Mr Naidoo's Hundredth Birthday

Before you read

1   This story focuses on a crime committed by a seemingly ordinary man. Are people who commit crimes always evil? Why do people commit crimes? Discuss your ideas with the rest of your class.

What's it about?

Read the story and answer questions 2 and 3 by yourself. Then discuss your answers with a partner.

2   The story is told by a first-person narrator. Write two sentences explaining the style of his language and what you think it suggests about him. Write down some quotations from the text to support your answer.

3   The narrator gives both facts and his opinions about Boola. Scan the first four pages of the story and list the facts and opinions that the reader is given in two columns.

Thinking about the text

4   Norman Silver is a skilled writer for young people. Explain in your own words how the story is designed to appeal to its audience by finishing off the sentences below:
   - The character of the narrator is designed to appeal to young people because . . .
   - The language of the narrator is appropriate for teenagers today because . . .
   - The character of Boola is engaging because . . .
   - The finding of the thumb is a good end to the story's mystery because . . .

5   It is clear from the narrator's language and descriptions of Boola that he liked him. Imagine you are the narrator. Write a formal letter to the authorities explaining the reasons for Boola's actions; persuade them that he should be treated with compassion despite his crime. Use evidence from the text to support the facts you include in your letter. Think carefully about persuasive techniques to support your argument.

Three poems by Choman Hardi

Before you read

1   Draw a spider diagram to show the cultures and traditions that have contributed to your upbringing. Ideas to consider include:
   ● the cultural diversity of where you live
   ● the cultural backgrounds of members of your family
   ● religion
   ● the influence of popular culture in the country where you live
   ● the food you eat.

What's it about?

Read the poems and answer questions 2 to 4 by yourself. Then discuss your answers in a small group.

2   *Life for Us* looks at how men and women were treated differently in the poet's childhood, for cultural reasons. List the differences the poet describes, then write a sentence explaining why you think she jumped into the water.

3   Write a paragraph to explain the significance of the title *The Middle Way*.

4   Write a paragraph to explain in your own words the feelings of the poet in *My Children*. Why do you think the poem ends with a question?

Thinking about the text

5   In *Life for Us* the writer chooses words and phrases carefully to help the reader to understand her envy of the male holidaymakers and the pleasure of jumping into the pool. In a two-column table, list the words and phrases the writer uses, and explain how they help the reader to understand the writer's feelings.

6   *The Middle Way* and *My Children* are about the tensions caused by combining cultures. What tensions can arise between children and parents as a result of their cultural differences? Discuss your ideas with the rest of your class, then get into a small group and write and perform a role play showing the tensions that can arise.

Robert and the Dog

Before you read

1   Discuss the two questions below with a partner. Then write down your answers. Begin your sentences with 'Every child/animal has the right to . . . '
    ● What are the five most important human rights for any child?
    ● What are the five most important animal rights for pets / kept animals?

What's it about?

Read the story and answer questions 2 to 4 by yourself. Then discuss your answers in a small group.

2   Write a short paragraph to explain what the text implies about the way Robert has been treated in his previous households. Use quotations from the story to support your answer.

3   Identify the sentence on page 37 that is the turning point in the story in terms of Robert's attitude to the family.

4   'Who born dog?' Explain in your own words what Robert's question means and why he is asking it.

Thinking about the text

5   'He gave the milk and dog food to his children when he got home.'
    a   What is your personal response to the penultimate line of the story? Write a paragraph describing this and how you feel about Robert.
    b   Look at the relationship between this line and the final line of the story. What do you think it shows about the author's perspective on the events of the story? Write a sentence or two explaining your answer.

6   What do you imagine Robert might say when he is challenged by his master about his actions? With a partner, devise a role play conversation between the two men. You might like to perform this to the rest of your class.

In the Name of My Father

Before you read

1   As this text shows, we can inherit much more from our parents than just physical characteristics. Discuss questions a and b with a partner.

   a   What characteristics have you inherited from your parents/ guardians or relatives?

   b   What characteristics, interests or behaviour of your family members / guardians would you be proud to carry forward into your adult life?

What's it about?

Read the article and answer questions 2 to 4 by yourself. Then discuss your answers in a small group.

2   **a**   The first two paragraphs of this newspaper article focus on personal loss. How does the writer's language and description convey a powerful sense of his loss?

   b   If the first two paragraphs focus on personal loss, what is the focus of paragraph 3?

3   'By exposing the double standards of oil companies who preached sound ecological virtues in the north while singing from an entirely different songsheet in Nigeria, my father earned powerful enemies'. Explain in your own words the meaning of Wiwa's point.

4   Explain in a sentence why Ken Wiwa was sent to private school in England.

Thinking about the text

5   Whilst the focus of this article is on the life and achievements of Ken Saro-Wiwa, we also learn a lot about his son, the writer. Select five quotations that you think reveal the character and emotions of Ken Wiwa and explain why you have chosen them. You may wish to list your selection in a table under the headings 'Quotation' and 'What this suggests about Ken Wiwa's character and emotions'.

6   This text considers the importance of his father to Ken Wiwa. In a small group, discuss the phrase 'following in your father's foot- steps'. Then write and perform a role play that is based on this idea.

A Place to Call Home

Before you read

1   Think about your bedroom. Describe it to a partner who has not seen it: pick out three features and explain what they reveal about your character.

What's it about?

Read the extract and answer questions 2 and 3 by yourself. Then compare your answers with a partner's.

2   Some teenagers might find the story about the cow (pages 48–49) upsetting but Roy and Simon Armitage don't appear to. What does Armitage suggest about Roy, and farmers in general, through his comments, tone and language?

3   Armitage describes the house in Luddenden Foot as if it was a crime scene. Why does he do this? Pick out two quotations from the text to support your answer.

Thinking about the text

4   The author chooses to use the second-person pronoun ('you') to write this non-fiction piece. Read his comments below from Chapter 1 of *All Points North*, then explain in your own words why he has chosen to adopt this writing style.

   We're a mixed bunch, although it's all relative, and one of us is no more mixed and no less relative than the rest. Me. On the other hand, sometimes it's somebody else. Those mixed-up days when it's easier to spot yourself in a crowd than recognise yourself in a mirror. On those occasions, it isn't me doing the rounds, getting about, going here, there and everywhere, but it isn't some stranger either. It's the other person, the second one. It's you.

5   Write your own observational piece on something or someone in your own life that is slightly comic and frustrating. You could choose one of the ideas below, or make up your own topic:
   - My father and the computer
   - Supermarket checkouts
   - My pet hate (in the style of the TV programme *Room 101*)

Compare and contrast

1   Many texts in this section explore parent–child relationships. Choose three or more relevant texts and discuss with a partner:
    ● the kind of relationship described
    ● whether it is fiction, non-fiction or poetry
    ● how the writer conveys the experience to the reader using any of the following elements: language, structure, setting, characterisation, events
    ● whether the experience is linked to the country the text is from and, if so, how
    ● why you found the text particularly interesting.

2   *Out of Bounds, Mr Naidoo's Hundredth Birthday* and *Robert and the Dog* describe the effect of poverty on particular people. Choose two of these, then copy and complete the table below. Use quotations to support your answers.

	Text 1	Text 2
Who is affected by poverty?		
How do we know?		
How does poverty affect the character's actions?		
What social or political issue is the writer encouraging the reader to think about?		

3   There are two pairings of texts by country in this section of the anthology. *Out of Bounds* and *Mr Naidoo's Hundredth Birthday* highlight issues related to South Africa; *Robert and the Dog* and *In the Name of My Father* focus on Nigeria. Select one of these pairings and write two paragraphs on what you have learned about the history or culture of the country and how this relates to the text. You might like to write about one or more of the following elements:

    characters   setting   language   events   author's viewpoint

4   Several of the texts in this section address the subject of love or friendship. Select two stories that convey a relationship that you find interesting and use the following questions to compare them.

- What relationship is described?
- How does the text convey the love/friendship? Is there a significant moment or turning point in this love/friendship?
- What is the writer's viewpoint about this relationship? Is the writer using the relationship to convey any social or cultural messages?
- Why did you choose this relationship to write about?

5 Imagine your class is putting together a school anthology of writing from around the world and can choose only one of the texts from this section to include. These are your selection criteria:
   - texts that appeal to young people and are a 'good read'
   - texts that give readers an insight into a range of cultures
   - texts that give readers the chance to discuss important social issues.

   Choose one of the stories that you have read so far and write a brief speech to argue the case for the text of your choice. It is essential to use evidence from the text to show how your choice fits the criteria above, and to give your personal response to the text.

2 Violence, war and death

The texts in this section all deal with the effect of violence and death on adults and children. Death is a natural part of human existence. However, many of these texts also reflect on the cruelty of mankind, which is often seen as a result of politics or war. The texts explore the points of view both of the victims of war and violence, and of those who inflict suffering on others. The first story even considers the point of view of the character of Death himself.

Activities

1   Different cultures make different associations with colours and symbols. In India, for example, red is connected with purity and used during weddings, and white is connected with mourning. White is also associated with mourning and death in China. What images and colours do you associate with death? Write down or draw your own ideas and then discuss them with a partner.

2   Think about a time when you were afraid and share your experience with the rest of your class. Use these questions to organise your thoughts:
   - Why were you frightened?
   - How did fear make your body feel?
   - Were you right about what might happen in the end?
   - Was there a happy ending?

3   a   Scan the front pages of today's newspapers and list any national or local examples of violence, war and death.

   b   Draw a table with the headings 'Incident' and 'Relevance to my life', and complete it using the examples you have found. Think about what relevance these incidents have to your own life. Then discuss your findings with a partner.

The Hunting of Death (Rwanda)

retold by Geraldine McCaughrean

A myth is a story that tries to interpret some aspect of the world around us. The tradition of literature from Rwanda is largely an oral one and little is written down; this myth has been retold in English by Geraldine McCaughrean, a children's author from England.

Rwanda is a small country in central Africa. It is currently very poor and its people have had to accept death as a fact of everyday life. Although this story is from many years ago, it is relevant to the Rwanda of today because its people have suffered greatly in recent years. In 1994 the Rwandan genocide (the systematic and planned killing of an entire national, racial, political, or ethnic group of people) resulted in the deaths of over one million people. By the time politicians in other countries considered trying to do anything about what was happening, it was too late.

At the start, God thought the world of his people: their smiles, their dancing, their songs. He did not wish them any harm in the world. So when he looked down and saw something scaly and scuttling darting from nook to cranny, he gave a great shout.

'People of Earth, look out! There goes Death! He will steal your heartbeat if you let him! Drive him out into the open, where my angels can kill him!' And fifty thousand angels flew down, with spears, clubs, drums and nets, to hunt down Death.

All through the world they beat their skin drums, driving Death ahead of them like the last rat in a cornfield. Death tried to hide in a bird's nest at the top of a tree; he tried to burrow in the ground. But the birds said, 'Away! God warned us of you!' And the animals said, 'Shoo! Be off with you!'

Closer and closer came the army of angel hunters. Their beating drums drove Death out of the brambles and tangles, out of the trees and the shadows of the trees, on to the sunny plain. There he came, panicked and panting, to a village.

He scratched at doors, tapped at windows, trying to get out of the glare of the sun, trying to get in and hide. But the people drove him away with brooms. 'Go away, you nasty thing! God warned us about you!'

The angel huntsmen were close to his heels when Death came to a field, where an old lady was digging.

'Oh glorious, lovely creature!' panted Death. 'I have run many miles across this hard world, but never have I seen such a beauty as you! Surely my eyes were made for looking at you. Let me sit here on the ground and gaze at you!'

The old lady giggled. 'Ooooh! What a flatterer you are, little crinkly one!'

'Not at all! I'd talk to your father at once and ask to marry you, but a pack of hunters is hard on my heels!'

'I know, I heard God say,' said the old woman. 'You must be that Death he talked of.'

'But *you* wouldn't like me to be killed, would you – a woman of your sweet nature and gentle heart? A maiden as lovely as you would never wish harm on a poor defenceless creature!' The drum beats came closer and closer.

The old woman simpered. 'Oh well. Best come on in under here,' she said and lifted her skirt, showing a pair of knobbly knee-caps. In out of the sunlight scuttled Death, and twined himself, thin and sinuous,[1] round her legs.

The angel huntsmen came combing the land, the line of them stretching from one horizon to the other. 'Have you seen Death pass this way?'

'Not I,' answered the old lady, and they passed on, searching the corn ricks, burning the long grass, peering down the wells. Of course, they found no trace of Death.

Out he came from under her skirts, and away he ran without a backward glance. The old woman threw a rock after him, and howled, 'Come back! Stop that rascal, God! Don't let him get away! He said he'd marry me!'

But God was angry. 'You sheltered Death from me when I hunted him. Now I shan't shelter you from him when he comes hunting for your heartbeat!' And with that he recalled[2] his angel huntsmen to Heaven.

And since then no angel has ever lifted her skirts to hide one of us, not one, until Death has passed by, hunting heartbeats.

Further reading

If you want to read more myths from around the world, try *Golden Myths and Legends of the World* or *Silver Myths and Legends of the World*, both by Geraldine McCaughrean (Orion Children's Books, 1999). The same author has also written *100 World Myths and Legends* (Orion Children's Books, 2001).

---

[1]**sinuous**   curving
[2]**recalled**   called back

Cassien's Story (Rwanda)

by Cassien Mbanda

Rwanda is a beautiful country in central Africa, known as the 'Land of a Thousand Hills'. It has a population of around 6 million people, made up of three main social groupings: the majority Hutu, the Tutsi[1] and the Twa. During a period of 100 days from 7 April to 16 July 1994, 1 million Tutsis and some moderate Hutus were killed in the Rwandan genocide (the systematic and planned killing of an entire national, racial, political, or ethnic group of people).

This non-fiction text was written by a Rwandan boy who was ten years old at the time of the genocide. A Tutsi, he lived with his parents, two sisters and a brother in Rwanda's capital, Kigali, where he attended primary school. After losing almost his entire family in the genocide, the organisation Survivors Fund (SURF) helped him rebuild his life. Cassien is just one of the thousands of survivors that SURF supports.

Cassien Mbanda

---

[1]**Tutsi**   cattle-raising people of Rwanda and Burundi

I was in Bicumbi visiting my grandmother and cousins when the genocide began. We hid in a nearby farm but were found by a group of local Hutumen.[2] I managed to escape, and hid in the bush, but my grandmother and cousins were not as lucky.

I joined the fleeing masses, walking all night, finally approaching the swamp at Rugende. But the *Interahamwe*[3] had set up a roadblock. Immediately they began shooting at us. We ran and struggled through the swamp. We hid in the bushes, and managed to stay hidden and would forage for food.

After a time I decided to seek refuge in the home of a family friend. But they informed the *Interahamwe* so I was forced to flee again. This time I did not escape. I was caught and hit with clubs and left for dead. But I survived.

I was found by a group of men and taken to a clinic, where I was treated. I had a broken leg, broken arm, and my head was covered in wounds too. But it was too dangerous to stay. Under the cover of darkness I escaped to my grandmother's house.

I collapsed, and awoke to find a soldier standing over me. He led me into the bush. I did not know if he planned to kill me. But when I saw other soldiers and they gave me some ripe bananas to eat, for the first time since the genocide had started, I began to feel safe.

I slowly recovered, and when the genocide ended I began to attend school again. I still could not walk properly. Soon after, two European women came to the school offering help for children who were severely ill or injured in the genocide. They took us to a nunnery at Byumba, from where we travelled to Kampala and then with a group of 90 children on to Italy.

We stayed in a military hospital, where doctors helped me to recover. After three months, I was taken to an orphanage with only Rwandan children to complete my primary education. Altogether I was in Italy for almost a year, and was able to

---

[2]**Hutumen**   men of the Bantu farming people of Rwanda and Burundi

[3]*Interahamwe*   a terrorist organisation that seeks to overthrow the government dominated by Tutsis and to reinstate Hutu control

speak fluent Italian. During a visit to London, I even met the Queen of England. It was an incredible experience.

A key turning point happened one Friday afternoon. I was told I was due to return to Rwanda, as one of my aunts, who had survived the genocide, had been located. Part of me was happy and wanted to go back to Rwanda. But it happened so suddenly I didn't even take any addresses of my friends.

I was happy to see my aunt and my surviving siblings, who had begun to attend school thanks to FARG (a government organisation to help survivors) who paid their fees.

However, my troubles had not totally ended. One day I started to get headaches. I couldn't read and I found it hard to concentrate. Despite painkillers the headaches wouldn't go away and I had to drop out of school.

However, help was at hand. I learned of an organisation called the Survivors Fund (SURF), which helps, supports and represents survivors of the genocide. It has an office in Kigali, and in London too. I was able to talk to them about my experiences, and they have helped me to rebuild my life.

However, I still sometimes feel sad that I had to leave Italy. But I also feel happy to be back in Rwanda and at home, having been able to find my siblings and just to be there for them.

Further reading

For more true children's stories from around the world, visit the BBC World Service website at

http://www.bbc.co.uk/worldservice/people/features/childrensrights/

Snipers (England)

by Roger McGough

In this poem, the narrator relates his memories of his uncle, who had fought in Burma against the Japanese in World War II and was haunted by what he had experienced.

When I was kneehigh to a tabletop,
Uncle Tom came home from Burma.
He was the youngest of seven brothers
so the street borrowed extra bunting[1]
and whitewashed him a welcome.

---

[1] **bunting**   patriotic and festive decorations made from cloth or paper, usually in the form of draperies or wide streamers

All the relations made the pilgrimage,
including us, laughed, sang, made a fuss.
He was as brown as a chairleg,
drank tea out of a white mug the size of my head,
and said next to nowt.

But every few minutes he would scan
the ceiling nervously, hands begin to shake.
'For snipers,' everyone later agreed,
'A difficult habit to break.'

Sometimes when the two of us were alone,
he'd have a snooze after dinner
and I'd keep an eye open for Japs.
Of course, he didn't know this
and the tanner² he'd give me before I went
was for keeping quiet,
but I liked to think it was money well spent.

Being Uncle Tom's secret bodyguard
had its advantages, the pay was good
and the hours were short, but even so,
the novelty soon wore off, and instead,
I started school and became an infant.

Later, I learned that he was in a mental home.
'Needn't tell anybody . . . Nothing serious
. . . Delayed shock . . . Usual sort of thing
. . . Completely cured now the doctors say.'
The snipers came down from the ceiling
but they didn't go away.

Over the next five years they picked off
three of his brothers; one of whom was my father.
No glory, no citations,³
Bang! straight through the heart.

---

²**tanner**   old sixpence
³**citations**   official commendations

Uncle Tom's married now, with a family.
He doesn't say much, but each night after tea,
he still dozes fitfully in his favourite armchair.
He keeps out of the sun, and listens now and then
for the tramp tramp tramp of the Colonel Bogeymen.
He knows damn well he's still at war,
just that the snipers aren't Japs anymore.

Further reading

If you enjoyed this, have a look at some more of Roger McGough's poetry. Two books that offer a selection of his poems are *All the Best: The Selected Poems of Roger McGough* (Puffin, 2004) and *Collected Poems* (Penguin, 2004).

Cut Me, and I Bleed Khaki[1] (England)

by Terence Blacker

This story focuses on a boy's relationship with his father and the
effect of war on their lives. The end of the story is set in the battle of
Caen, which was a battle between Allied and German forces during
World War II's Battle of Normandy. This took place from June to
August 1944.

Cagny, France, July 1944

You can kill almost anything when you are at war but you can't
kill a ghost.

Ghosts belong in old country houses with creaky floor-
boards and hidden stairways. They are for times when fear is
something freakish and unusual. At a moment like this, when
it is in the air that you breathe night and day, they are the very
last thing you would expect to see. Ghosts have no place when
the living are trying to kill one another.

And yet I saw one. The ghost was there in front of me,
standing, wide-eyed, in a thicket at the end of a lane. We stared
at each other, him and me, for ten seconds, twenty, more. I felt
my hand, clammy with sweat on the trigger of my machine-gun.
Then, as he gazed into my eyes, I knew, I understood. I relaxed.

I haven't told the lads about the ghost, and I probably
never will, even if I return home alive after this lark.

In the six weeks of action since we landed on that beach in
Normandy, I've discovered that soldiers can talk about missing
home and their girlfriends, they can be rude about the officers
or make jokes about the enemy, but there is one thing that is
never mentioned and that is fear.

Fear makes you weak and, in war, weakness kills.

So I shall write it down. As I sit, leaning against an apple
tree, warmed by the evening sun, I gaze at the notebook my

---

[1]**khaki**   a dull yellowish-brown colour, often used for military clothing

mother gave me for my fourteenth birthday, its black leather cover bent and stained by the sweat of war.

Most of the boys are catching up on some shut-eye under a hedge nearby. Today is the first time for almost a week that we have been able to spend time out of our tanks and rest. We've certainly found ourselves a cushy billet² in this little orchard. No tanks have churned up the grass and crushed the trees, no shells have pitted the ground. It is the end of a still summer's day, a blackbird is singing in a tree and the sun is high in the sky. If it were not for the rumble of artillery on the horizon, the scene might almost be normal.

But some of us, even after two solid days of fighting, are unable to close our eyes. In a far corner, I can see our squadron leader Major Bathurst as he writes to the mothers, fathers and wives of those who have died over the past week. One or two of the men have found themselves a quiet tree and are writing home.

Under a cherry tree near to where I am sitting, Sergeant 'Mosh' McMullen sits gazing across the fields as if, at any moment, enemy tanks might appear. He catches me looking at him and allows a rare smile to flicker across his face.

Yesterday, after the business with the Tiger, it was the sergeant who took me aside.

'Today, Skinny,' he said, 'you became a man. You became a soldier.'

I smiled, shrugged modestly, like a man, like a soldier, should. 'Thanks, Sarge,' I said.

Maybe he was right. But if he was, how is it that right now I feel like a child?

At times likes this, I think of my father, Sergeant Danvers. How would he be now, resting after battle? In my mind, I can see him, small, broad-shouldered, his eyes narrowed against the evening sun.

---

²**billet**   place for a soldier to live

Little soldier. For as long as I could remember, that was what he called me. Back from exercises[3] or from drill at the barracks, he would stride into the bungalow where we lived, give my mum a kiss, then turn his attention to me.

In the early days, we would play the same game every day.

When I heard him open the front door, I would hide under the kitchen table. He would come in, chat away, until I made a noise.

'Sssh!' he would say suddenly. 'Did you hear something, Mrs Danvers? I'm sure I heard a noise.'

Beneath the table, I would move again, giggle.

'I did. It's a burglar!' And he would be down upon me, grabbing me, tickling me, rolling across the floor, hugging me with mock ferocity. 'Here he is! I've got him! He's a strong little thing, Mrs Danvers. He's a little soldier.'

Then, after a minute or so, it would suddenly be over. 'There you go, little soldier.'

He would stand up, ruffle my hair, and slip back into the mysterious world of grown-ups, hardly speaking to me until it was time for me to go to bed when, a glass of whisky in his hand, he would wink at me. 'Night, son.'

On my fifth birthday, my father gave me a pair of boxing-gloves. He slipped them on to my hands, tightened the laces on my wrist and sat forwards in the kitchen chair. 'Have a go then, son. Give me an old straight left to the face.' I can see his wide smile now as he presented me with his face, my target.

I drew my left arm back and punched him, fast and strong, on the point of his nose. To my horror, a terrible sound, a sort of wet muffled crack, could be heard. My father put his hands to his lower face.

When he lowered them, blood was trickling from both nostrils, down over his upper lip, reddening his teeth.

'You little devil, you.' He stood up, walked to the sink and dabbed at his nose with a cloth.

---

[3]**exercises**   military practice

'Jim.' My mother stood at the door, looking worried. 'Jim, don't get angry. It wasn't his fault.'

'Hold your tongue, woman.' He sat back down on the chair in front of me. His nose was red and swollen.

At that time, I was not afraid of my father. I respected him. He was a soldier in the best tank regiment in the army, a sergeant. He was my dad. Sometimes he shouted at my mum but he was not really a fearsome figure, then.

So it was only because I was upset that I had hurt my dad that made tears well up in my eyes.

'Oh no, boy.' A look of annoyance now clouded my father's face. 'Don't go and spoil it. You landed a good punch on me.' He put his face close to mine so that I could see a thin trace of blood emerging from one of his nostrils. 'Enjoy it, little soldier. Enjoy it while you can.'

He untied the gloves, pulled them off my hands and returned them to a drawer. I never saw them again.

We moved around. Catterick, Aldershot, Tidworth, Lisburn. As an army kid, you get used to being on your own, to knowing that friendship is something which lasts one or two years at the most.

And my father, somehow, became less Dad and more Sergeant Danvers with every year. I missed the smell of whisky on his breath when he kissed me goodnight. Sometimes it felt as if the last time I had touched him had been when I had landed that punch on his nose on my fifth birthday.

He would go away for weeks on exercises, returning grim-faced and silent, laughing only when I asked where he had been. 'Can't tell you that, boy,' he would say. 'Can't risk national security because a snot-nosed ten-year-old is too curious for his own good.'

'He was only being interested,' my mother would murmur.

And my father would look at her with a cold glance that suggested it was a waste of his precious energy even to answer her. We were background on those occasions. Beside the great matter of the war that was approaching, the everyday things of my life – school, sport, teachers – were trivial.

'We'll be fighting for freedom. Think of that, boy. The future of Europe is in our hands.'

Once, a few months before the war began, I asked him whether he was ever afraid. He looked at me with disappointment, almost disgust.

'You're frit aren't you, boy. Frit that Jerry is going to take you away from your mummy.'

I shook my head.

'The army would make a man of you. Would you like that?'

I nodded, not knowing quite what to say.

'I doubt it. I very much doubt it.'

One night, my father returned late from the sergeants' mess. He must have been drinking but his voice sounded different, less angry than usual. It was excited, almost boyish. 'Mobilisation.' He spoke as if the word which would take soldiers to war were the most beautiful in the English language. 'At last, we're seeing action.'

Between sobs, my mother said something about being afraid, about feeling lonely without him.

'Don't talk soft, woman. You'll only make it worse for yourself. You'll have the kid for company.'

My mother continued crying.

He never spoke to me about leaving – war, I suppose, was not something children were meant to understand – but three weeks later, he left for France. I remember seeing him rumbling out of the barracks, his head poking out of the turret of a Matilda.[4] One tank. I called out to him as he roared past but he stared ahead of him, eyes squinting in the bright sunlight. I never saw him again.

They called it the phoney war, those first few months when the British Expeditionary Force was in France but never engaging with the enemy, but they felt pretty real to my mother and me.

---

[4]**Matilda**   a $26\frac{1}{2}$ ton British tank of early World War II, having a crew of four and armed with a 40mm gun

Now and then, we would get a postcard. My mother would read them over and over again to me, but the words in them – Keeping our spirits up . . . feeling a little the worse for wear after exercises . . . last night we raised a glass to the folks at home – sounded like somebody else's.

Among the army wives, there were rumours of where the regiment was based in France but, because no one was meant to know about things, the news was whispered guiltily as if German spies were earwigging[5] on every corner of the married quarters.

It was a quiet time, and one that I secretly enjoyed, but soon the newspapers were full of news from the front. The phoney war was over and the real one had begun.

On the afternoon of 5th June 1940, I opened the front door after school, took one glance at the scene in the kitchen and knew what had happened. My mother sat at the kitchen table, holding her head in her hands as if in prayer. Standing behind her, an arm resting on her shoulder, was our neighbour Mrs Bullen.

'Hullo, Steve,' she said in a soft voice.

My mother looked up and said, in a strangely polite voice, almost as if she was talking to an interviewer on the wireless, 'Stephen, your father is missing in action. The War Office have sent us a telegram.'[6]

I must have looked confused because Mrs Bullen began to explain, 'That means – '

'He knows what it means.' Mum spoke as if there were no life left in her, either. 'He's an army kid.'

I moved across the kitchen and put my arm awkwardly around her shoulder. She leant away from me. For some inexplicable reason, I felt that she was blaming me for everything that had happened.

Soon, around the married quarters at our barracks, it wasn't unusual to have lost a dad. During that spring, the time of

---

[5]**earwigging**   listening in
[6]**telegram**   message sent by telegraph, often used for urgent matters

Dunkirk, hardly a week went by without another boy or girl in my class getting the bad news. Usually, the first we would know about it would be an empty desk in the classroom. Then, when they returned, nobody would say anything about it although everyone would know. It was like being the member of a club that no one wanted to belong to.

Time heals, they say – but they're wrong. It just makes the pain different, turns it into a dull, ever-present ache of loneliness. The war went on. Sometimes people would talk about the 'miracle of Dunkirk', of how thousands of British soldiers were rescued from the beach in northern France by a fleet of little boats that crossed the Channel, but for me there was no miracle. My father was gone. It was only when he was no longer there that I began to realize how important he was to me.

I knew I was supposed to be grown-up – I turned 14 in 1942 and was tall for my age – but I felt as if my father had gone before I had had time to talk to him.

'The army's my family,' he used to say. 'If you cut me, I'd bleed khaki.'

I began to wonder about that. What was so wrong with his real family that it had to take second place to the army?

I had always thought that there would come a day when I could look him in the eye and prove to him that he could be proud of me. Now that day would never come.

My mother was braver than me. She found a job in an armaments[7] factory. She went out with her friends. When a boy at school mentioned that he had seen her in the passenger seat of a jeep driven by an airman from a nearby American base, I realized that she didn't need me at home any more.

And I knew what I had to do.

One dark morning in January 1943, I let myself out of the house before my mother had awoken. Over my shoulder was an old kit bag that I had found in the cupboard under the stairs

---

[7]**armaments**   military weapons and apparatus

and had filled with a few clothes. I walked down the road and took the bus into town. I was going to war.

Without anyone knowing it, my school had helped me become a soldier. There had been a poster in the corridor, meant for older boys, which had the address of the recruiting[8] office of the 23rd Hussars. Maps in Geography had shown me how to get to my destination. The pens in Art had helped me change one small detail on my birth certificate. The year in which I was born changed from 1928 to 1926.

The sergeant behind the desk, a small man with a bent, boxer's nose, glanced at my papers, then up at me. For a moment, he seemed to be considering whether to ask me a few questions but then he thought better of it. It wasn't difficult to join the war effort at that time. I was a soldier at last.

Six months into my training, I knew that I was in the best regiment in the British army. The 23rd Hussars had been set up in 1941 which meant that we didn't have the history, the tradition, the old comrades of other regiments. No one had stories about the way army life had been in the old days because almost all of the men had been civilians until they joined up.

In B Squadron, my outfit, we had a cobbler,[9] a vet, an accountant and all number of factory or farm workers. Some of the men were in their late thirties and had never thought they would fight. A few were in their teens, although none of them was as young as I was.

Sometimes on exercises we would meet blokes from other regiments. They would be full of boasts and stories about their outfit. Those of us in the 23rd may not have had the airs and graces of those in flashier regiments but we had spirit and some of the best, bravest lads you could ever hope to meet.

The training was hard. There were moments – soaked to the skin in a funk-hole on the Yorkshire moors, hungry and freezing cold in the darkness of the hull of my tank – when I

---

[8]**recruiting**   joining the armed forces
[9]**cobbler**   person who makes and mends footwear

cursed myself for walking away from the comfort of my home that early morning.

As for Mum, I tried not to think of her but wrote a single card in May 1944 when all the talk was of a big push into Europe. I told her I was fine, that I was serving my country and that she could be proud of me.

Two weeks later we rumbled out of the barracks and headed for the south coast. It was time to go to war.

In the hull of the Sherman tank, you are in your own world, dark and sealed up. Inside it reeks of grease and human sweat. In summer, you bake; in winter, the cold reaches into the marrow of your bones. The only people who truly exist for you are the members of your crew.

Major Bathurst, squadron leader.

Sergeant Mosh McMullen, wireless operator.

Corporal Billy Sims, corporal gunner.

Trooper Johnny 'Titch' Garrett, driver.

And then there was me – no longer 'the kid' but Trooper Steve 'Skinny' Danvers, co-driver, hull machine-gunner, tea-maker.

Beyond that darkness, different kinds of hell can be breaking loose but, to stay sane, you don't think about the horrors of that world outside. You drive, you fire your 75mm. You don't think of the death or injury that, at any moment, could be hurtling towards you.

For three weeks, we were part of a huge traffic-jam of tanks, half-tracks, self-propelled artillery, scout cars and ambulances, hemmed in by the presence of enemy troops some six miles from the Normandy beach where we landed.

One day historians will tell the story of how, on 26th June 1944, the 11th Armoured Division, including the 23rd Hussars, played their part in the battle for Normandy. The truth is, I remember little and sometimes what I do recall I wish I could forget.

Before dawn, the sky behind was a flickering red inferno of artillery as the 600 guns of the Second Army opened up from behind the lines to 'soften up' the enemy who were ahead of us. As we waited in our tanks, it was the first time for most of us that we heard the rushing hiss of shells as they flew over our heads, the echoing thud as they exploded two miles away.

Soon after first light, the infantry who were to lead the attack, the 15th Scottish infantry, rose to their feet and marched into the battle from which most of them would never return.

Then, with a roar of engines, it was our turn. Even before a shot had been fired at us, we realized that this was going to be different from any exercise back home. We were used to moors and plains. Here the countryside consisted of small fields surrounded by steep banks that our tanks climbed, rocking back almost to a perpendicular position before crashing downwards on the other side.

At home, there had been mud. Here, a fine grey dust enveloped every vehicle, clogging the eyes, choking the lungs.

There was no time for fear. Even when we first engaged with the Germans' huge Tiger and Panther tanks, our only thought was for the next action: advance, attack, divert, fire, survive.

Battle changes a person for ever. There were tragedies during the next few days, acts of heroism and comradeship which only someone who has fought could truly understand. Yet, when we were withdrawn and had time to gather around the graves of dead friends – B Squadron had been badly knocked about while trying to take a hill called Point 112 – each of us had only one thought. We have taken what they could throw us. We have come through. There was no excitement about this, no bragging, but a sort of hard, dead-eyed confidence. We weren't ex-civilians, kids or pensioners, the odds-and-sods brigade. We were soldiers.

My father was with me all of this time. Even when the artillery was thundering, when we were in the thick of it, the presence of Sergeant Danvers was there.

He was proud of me. I sensed that, too. And he was going to protect me from harm.

I have never been superstitious but I took it as a sign that, when we were joined by reinforcements from the 24th Lancers, one of them – a Trooper Terry Hagman – turned out to have known him back in 1940.

We were in slit-trench in the shade of a tank when Terry seemed to pick up my surname for the first time.

'Danvers?' He looked me hard in the eye. There was something sour and battle-weary about the man that I didn't quite trust. 'You any relation to Sergeant Jim Danvers?'

'He was my father,' I said.

'Knew him in France.' Hagman drew on his cigarette and gazed into the distance.

'He died there.'

'I heard.'

Mosh McMullen must have noticed that this mattered to me, that I needed to know more. 'Skinny wants to know how his dad died.'

'Yeah?' Hagman looked at his cigarette, enjoying the moment of drama. 'He was strafed[10] – machine-gunned – from the air,' he said casually. 'He died as he lived.'

I glanced at him and for a moment he seemed to be considering whether to tell me more about the way Sergeant Jim Danvers met his end, but I had heard enough.

'That's good.' I said. 'It's all I wanted to know.'

'You're right,' said Trooper Hagman. 'That's all you want to know.' And the conversation moved on.

Those first few days of battle had changed us more than months or years of training ever could. For the first time, we felt as if we were part of a great force, that we could win. We believed that, with the artillery behind us and the RAF boys supporting us from the air, we could do the job. It was not going to be

---

[10]**strafed**   attacked by aeroplanes with machine-gun fire

pleasant. Not all of us would see it through. But it would be done.

There were other things we had discovered. The German tanks, Tigers and Panthers, were bigger than ours, their armour was thicker and their guns had a longer range. Our Shermans were what we called 'quick brewers' – more than any other tanks, they burst into flames within moments of being hit. The greatest danger facing those of us inside was being burnt alive.

But now that we were in the thick of it, we didn't talk about the danger or the glory, death or victory. We simply concentrated on the next task ahead – a bridgehead to hold, a hill to defend, a ridge to be taken. Above all, we didn't think too much. Thinking was for later.

There was to be a big push – some of the lads had heard that it was going to be the biggest armoured advance of the war. 11th Armoured Division was to be in the group leading the attack across the cornfields south of Caen.

It was not a simple task. First of all, we had to cross a river at dead of night and with no radio contact in order to form up for battle on the far side. Then there was another little problem. The first thing that we would reach as we advanced would be an enemy minefield. Three lanes had been made through the mines and we were to follow those lanes. Only once we were through could we fan out and begin our advance in earnest. Our mission was to take a ridge seven miles into enemy territory.

We made the crossing and, at dawn on 18th July, a square mile of armoured vehicles sat, glinting in the sun, waiting for its moment. From behind us, we heard the distant hum of aircraft. Bomber Command was on its way to drop a heavy load on enemy positions four miles ahead of us. As great black Lancaster bombers, escorted by Spitfires, droned over our heads, we stood on our tanks and cheered. It was the moment of truth at last.

Before our eyes, the quiet landscape erupted under the bombardment – first of the Lancasters, then the medium bombers and finally under shellfire from artillery.

Then it was our turn. Beside me, Titch started up the engine, crews settled into their turrets. We moved forwards, slowly at first as we made our way in single file over the mine-field, then on at full tilt.

It was like driving over another planet. Everything living seemed to have been destroyed and was still smoking after attack from the air – cornfields, villages, churches, woods.

After a couple of miles, we reached the first of the German troops. Those that had survived the bombing and shelling were in no fit state to fight. Some were grey-faced zombies, stagger-ing past us, too dazed to be afraid. Others were still in their dug-outs but were shaking and shuddering from the shock of the bombardment.

'Poor beggars,' I called out to Titch as we thundered past.

He laughed as if I had made some kind of joke. 'They don't know what hit them,' he said.

We crossed one railway, then two. We were still a couple of miles from the ridge we were meant to be taking but suddenly we came under enemy fire. It was when we emerged from a small village that the major saw something that made him halt our progress.

Some 500 yards ahead of us, on an open plain, a squadron of tanks stood motionless. They were completely exposed to enemy fire, or at least they would have been were it not for the fact that the roar of anti-tank guns from the ridge ahead had fallen silent. There was something strange about the stillness of the scene, with the blanket of dust that had settled on the tanks making them look like ancient forgotten monuments in a grey desert.

The tanks were Shermans. Looking through his field-glasses, Major Bathurst told us they belonged to the Fife and Forfar, the regiment that had been leading us into battle. The question was: why had they stopped?

Standing on his tank, the major glanced at his watch. His orders had been to advance at speed but there was something about the sight ahead of us which worried him.

We heard his instructions through the headphones. 'Take a closer look at that, will you, Sergeant McMullen?'

The sergeant gave the order to move. 'Go easy, Titch,' he said.

Our tank moved away from B Squadron, out of cover and on to the sunlit plain. There was a lull in the battle and, as I gazed towards our destination, the sun was warm on my face.

Little soldier.

400 yards. 300. Now, in the shadow of one of the tanks, we saw signs of movement. 'Looks like they've been shot up.' The sergeant's voice was matter-of-fact. 'A couple of tanks have lost their tracks. We could be going through a minefield.'

Thanks for the good news, Sarge.

200 yards. 150.

Be alert, little soldier. The enemy can strike you at any time and from anywhere.

Something made me look to the right towards where the sun shone bright over a clump of blackened trees on some undulating ground.

Movement near a shell crater between us and the wood. It was a man who seemed to appear out of nowhere. Bare-headed, and so covered in grey dust that it was impossible to see what uniform he was wearing, he walked slowly, with a weaving stagger, towards us.

I levelled my machine gun at him, began to squeeze the trigger but the man kept on walking. I looked around me, to Titch, the sergeant behind me, but their attention was on the tanks ahead of us.

Then I realized that something very strange was happening. The Sherman was advancing, but the man's position in relation to us remained the same. For the first time, I could see his eyes in his mud-spattered face. They were an icy blue.

Did you hear something, Mrs Danvers? And suddenly I knew, as sure as I know that I am here, writing this to you, that he was back. Here, in the thick of battle, I was with my father again.

At this point, he raised both arms to me, as if imploring me for something, then half-turned towards the group of trees behind him, then back to me.

Something caught my eye in the wood. A glint of metal. There, almost entirely hidden by trees and a small dip in the ground, its gun moving downwards towards us, was a mighty German Tiger, crouching, waiting to attack.

It was the end. *Cut me, and I bleed khaki.*

There was no time to scream into the intercom. I opened fire with the machine gun. The sound echoed across the plain.

The rounds that I fired bounced off the armour of the tank but now all eyes were on it. Calmly, I heard Sergeant McMullen calling for covering fire from the 17 pounder. At the same time, Billy Sims opened up from behind me. There was no time to get inside our hatches. Seconds later, explosions from the wood buffeted our faces as we took cover in the tank like rabbits down a hole.

The bombardment continued for a minute, maybe longer, and for every second of it we expected the explosion from the Tiger that would send us into the next world.

Then, as if at a signal, silence. The sergeant's voice came over the air. 'Someone up there likes us,' he said.

We opened the hatch. There were several mighty shell craters where the German tank had been – but no Tiger.

'Scarpered[11] behind the hill,' said Sergeant McMullen. 'We won't be seeing them again.'

I remembered the man who had warned me. 'There's a survivor to our right, Sarge,' I said.

The sergeant halted the tank. 'Where was he, son?'

My eyes scanned the ground between where we stood and the wood. Open, dusty plain. There was no one there.

'He . . . he seems to have gone.'

'Battle fever, Skinny?' A day ago, the sergeant's voice would have been angry but there was respect there now. We made our

---

[11]**scarpered**   ran off

way forwards. An entire squadron of the Fifes had been knocked out. The things I saw over the next few minutes as we called up the ambulance and half-tracks to take away the survivors made me forget our own narrow squeak.

Now though, in the unearthly peace of this orchard, I think about my father and begin to understand how it must have been for him, trying to be a soldier and a father at a time of fear. He returned and, on that battlefield near Caen, he showed me how to be a man. He proved to his little soldier that, before anything else in the world, he was my dad.

It is time to write home to Mother and tell her that I am safe.

Further reading

You can find more information on child soldiers at
http://web.amnesty.org/pages/childsoldiers-index-eng

Other books about war that you might enjoy include *Goodnight Mr Tom* by Michelle Magorian (Longman, 1998), *Waiting for Anya* by Michael Morpurgo (Egmont Books, 2007) and *A Time of Fire* by Robert Westall (Catnip Publishing, 2007).

Barefoot Gen (Japan)

by Keiji Nakazawa

This text is a Japanese manga. Manga is one of the biggest publication industries in Japan: at the end of the 20th century, it made up about 40 per cent of the publications in Japan. It has also become increasingly popular in other countries. You may have seen manga for teenagers being sold in bookshops – Japanese is read from right to left, so many of the translations start at the back!

Barefoot Gen is the semi-autobiographical story of the artist Keiji Nakazawa. On the morning of 6 August 1945, when he was six

years old, something happened that changed his life for ever: an atomic bomb was used in war for the first time and normal life in the crowded Japanese city of Hiroshima came to a sudden and terrifying end. More than 70,000 people died and many more were injured. The heat of the blast was so intense that people at the centre of the explosion were simply vaporised. Many who survived the blast died later from the radiation.

The President of the USA, Harry Truman, warned the Japanese to surrender. When they did not, a second bomb was dropped on Nagasaki, killing around 40,000 people and wounding 60,000. Hiroshima was a turning point in our understanding of the fact that, without peace, we could destroy the whole human race.

Nakazawa lost his sister, father and brother to the bomb. This extract from *Barefoot Gen* describes the events immediately before, during and after the first bomb was dropped on Hiroshima. The full story is nearly 2,000 pages long. It was translated and published in English by a volunteer organisation, Project Gen.

UNAWARE OF THE HELL THAT WAS APPROACHING IN THE SKY, HIROSHIMA BEGAN THE DAY AS USUAL...

EXCUSE ME, YOUNG MAN...

YES, MA'AM?

SIGN: "KAMIYAMA NATIONAL ELEMENTARY SCHOOL"

IS THE FIRST GRADE CLASS HELD AT THE SCHOOL OR THE TEMPLE?

GEE, I DON'T KNOW... YOU'LL HAVE TO ASK THE TEACHER...

HEY!

IT'S A B-29!

WHEN DID *IT* GET HERE?

THAT'S STRANGE... THE SIRENS DIDN'T EVEN GO OFF...

THE FUSELAGE IS SHINING IN THE SUN...

ENOLA GAY

ALTITUDE 31,000 FEET-- *LET IT GO!*

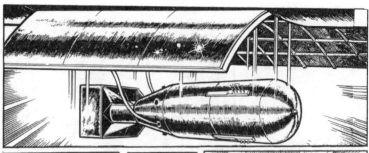

...THERE'S SOMETHING *WHITE* FALLING...

FLASH

43 SECONDS LATER, 1800 FEET OVER HIROSHIMA, THE ATOMIC BOMB NAMED "LITTLE BOY" EXPLODED WITH A WHITE-HOT LIGHT-- IT WAS AS IF A MILLION FLASH BULBS HAD GONE OFF AT ONCE...

FLASH

WH-O-O-OSH

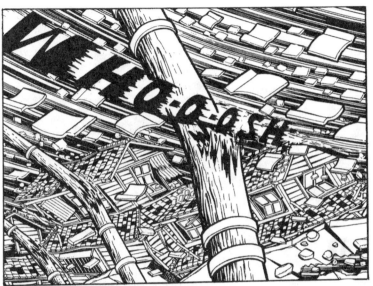

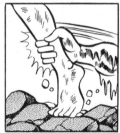

ARGH! WHAT DO YOU WANT? *LET GO* OF ME!!

SON... SONNY... BRING ME... *WATER*...

...PLEASE... ...PLEASE... MY THROAT IS *BURNING*... ...WATER...

HANG ON, MISTER, JUST HANG ON... I'LL GET SOME...

QUICK... ....QUICK...

FOR HOURS, GEN WANDERS ALONE THROUGH THE BURNING WRECKAGE OF HIROSHIMA, SEARCHING FOR HIS FAMILY...

SOMEWHERE IN THE FLAMES ARE HIS LITTLE BROTHER, HIS SISTER, FATHER, MOTHER, AND THE UNBORN CHILD SHE CARRIES....

...AS THEY ESCAPE THE FLAMES, GEN'S MOTHER GOES INTO LABOR, AND WITH NO ONE TO HELP THEM, THEY BRING A NEW LIFE INTO THE DYING CITY...

Further reading

An excellent summary of the history and importance of manga texts in Japan can be found at
http://www.animeinfo.org/animeu/hist102.html

A well-known Japanese animation linked to the manga form is called *Spirited Away*, which is available on DVD.

You can listen to the American president's announcement about the dropping of the bomb and a survivor's account at
http://archives.cbc.ca/IDD-1-71-1794/conflict_war/hiroshima/

Enola Gay (USA)

by Esther Morgan

Enola Gay is the B-29 Superfortress bomber that dropped 'Little Boy', the first atomic bomb ever used in warfare, when the United States Army Air Forces (USAAF) attacked Hiroshima, Japan, on 6 August 1945, just before the end of World War II. Because of its role in the atomic bombings of Japan, its name has become synonymous with the controversy over the bombings themselves. In this poem, Esther Morgan imagines the mother of the man who led the crew that dropped the bomb on Hiroshima. Colonel Paul Tibbets named the plane after his mother, Enola Gay Tibbets, and so her name too has become synonymous with this major event in history.

She could be anybody's mother
pegging out the washing on a hot August morning,
lifting a sheet's saintly dazzle to the line.

The day stretches in front of her stainlessly:
her hands keep her busy, fluttering through each room
until all the windows are blinding.

She irons away the long afternoon,
pressing summer dresses thin as her own skin,
her face blurred by the clouds of steam.

Evening and his bedtime comes around again:
she'd kiss him then tell him to *Blow out the light*,
flicking the switch to his breath.

She whispers his name before she falls asleep:
all night she flies for mile after starless mile
over fields of white linen.[1]

---

[1] **linen**   a fabric woven from fibres from the flax plant

Further reading

If you enjoyed this, you might like to read some more of Esther Morgan's poetry. You could start with *Beyond Calling Distance* (Bloodaxe Books, 2001) or *The Silence Living in Houses* (Bloodaxe Books, 2005). Another poet you might enjoy is Carol Ann Duffy – try *The World's Wife* (Picador, 2000).

Homage (South Africa)

by Nadine Gordimer

This is a disturbing, violent story which illustrates how people, when desperate, can be used and exploited by others. Much of Nadine Gordimer's writing is inspired by events in South Africa, where the political system of apartheid separated people according to the colour of their skin.

The story is told to us by a murderer, who has left his own country through desperation. The word 'homage' means paying respect to a person who is senior to you or in charge of you: in this case it could be the rich woman being watched by the narrator, or the people that have asked him to commit a crime.

Read my lips.

Because I don't speak. You're sitting there, and when the train lurches you seem to bend forward to hear. But I don't speak.

If I could find them I could ask for the other half of the money I was going to get when I'd done it, but they're gone. I don't know where to look. I don't think they're here, anymore, they're in some other country, they move all the time and that's how they find men like me. We leave home because of governments overthrown, a conscript[1] on the wrong side; no work, no bread or oil in the shops, and when we cross a border we're put over another border, and another. What is your final destination? We don't know; we don't know where we can stay, where we won't be sent on somewhere else, from one tent camp to another in a country where you can't get papers.

I don't ever speak.

They find us there, in one of these places – they found me and they saved me, they can do anything, they got me in here with papers and a name they gave me; I buried my name, no-one will ever dig it out of me. They told me what they wanted done and

---

[1] **conscript**   military term for someone who is compelled to enter military service

they paid me half the money right away. I ate and I had clothes to wear and I had a room in a hotel where people read the menu outside three different restaurants before deciding where to have their meal. There was free shampoo in the bathroom and the key to a private safe where liquor was kept instead of money.

They had prepared everything for me. They had followed him for months and they knew when he went where, at what time – although he was such an important man, he would go out privately with his wife, without his State bodyguards, because he liked to pretend to be an ordinary person or he wanted to be an ordinary person. They knew he didn't understand that that was impossible for him; and that made it possible for them to pay me to do what they paid me to do.

I am nobody; no country counts me in its census, the name they gave me doesn't exist: nobody did what was done. He took time off, with his wife by the arm, to a restaurant with double doors to keep out the cold, the one they went to week after week, and afterwards, although I'd been told they always went home, they turned into a cinema. I waited. I had one beer in a bar, that's all, and I came back. People coming out of the cinema didn't show they recognised him because people in this country like to let their leaders be ordinary. He took his wife, like any ordinary citizen, to that corner where the entrance goes down to the subway trains and as he stood back to let her pass ahead of him I did it. I did it just as they paid me to, as they tested my marksmanship for, right in the back of the skull. As he fell and as I turned to run, I did it again, as they paid me to, to make sure.

She made the mistake of dropping on her knees to him before she looked up to see who had done it. All she could tell the police, the papers and the enquiry was that she saw the back of a man in dark clothing, a leather jacket, leaping up the flight of steps that leads from the side-street. This particular city is one of steep rises and dark alleys. She never saw my face. Years later now, (I read in the papers) she keeps telling people how she never saw the face, she never saw the face of the one who did it, if only she had looked up seconds sooner – they would have been able to find me, the nobody who did it would have become me. She thinks all the time about the back of my head in the dark cap (it was not dark, really, it was a light green-and-brown check, an expensive cap I'd bought with the money, afterwards I threw it in the canal with a stone in it). She thinks of my neck, the bit of my neck she could have seen between the cap and the collar of the leather jacket (I couldn't throw that in the canal, I had it dyed). She thinks of the shine of the leather jacket across my shoulders under the puddle of light from a street-lamp that stands at the top of the flight, and my legs moving so fast I disappear while she screams.

The police arrested a drug-pusher they picked up in the alley at the top of the steps. She couldn't say whether or not it was him because she had no face to remember. The same with others the police raked in from the streets and from those with criminal records and political grievances;[2] no face. So I had nothing to fear. All the time I was being pushed out of one country into another I was afraid, afraid of having no papers, afraid of being questioned, afraid of being hungry, but now I had nothing to be afraid of. I still have nothing to fear. I don't speak.

I search the papers for whatever is written about what was done; the inquiry doesn't close, the police, the people, this whole country, keep on searching. I read all the theories; sometimes, like now, in the subway train, I make out on the back of someone's newspaper a new one. An Iranian plot, because of this country's hostility towards some government there. A South African attempt to revenge this country's sanctions against some racist government there, at the time. I could tell who did it, but not why. When they paid me the first half of the money – just like that, right away! – they didn't tell me and I didn't ask. Why should I ask; what government, on any side, anywhere, would take me in. They were the only people to offer me anything.

---

[2] **grievances** complaints

And then I got only half what they promised. And there isn't much left after five years, five years next month. I've done some sort of work, now and then, so no-one would be wondering where I got the money to pay the rent for my room and so on. Worked at the race course, and once or twice in night clubs. Places where they don't register you with any labour office. What was I thinking I was going to do with the money if I had got it all, as they promised? Get away, somewhere else? When I think of going to some other country, like they did, taking out at the frontier the papers and the name of nobody they gave me, showing my face –

I don't talk.

I don't take up with anybody. Not even a woman. Those places I worked, I would get offers to do things, move stolen goods, handle drugs: people seemed to smell out somehow I'd made myself available. But I am not! I am not here, in this city. This city has never seen my face, only the back of a man leaping up the steps that led to the alley near the subway station. It's said, I know, that you return to the scene of what you did. I never go near, I never walk past that subway station. I've never been back to those steps. When she screamed after me as I disappeared, I disappeared for ever.

I couldn't believe it when I read that they were not going to bury him in a cemetery. They put him in the bit of public garden in front of the church that's near the subway station. It's an ordinary-looking place with a few old trees dripping in the rain on gravel paths, right on a main street. There's an engraved stone and a low railing, that's all. And people come in their lunch-hour, people come while they're out shopping, people come up out of that subway, out of that cinema, and they tramp over the gravel to go and stand there, where he is. They put flowers down.

I've been there. I've seen. I don't keep away. It's a place like any other place, to me. Every time I go there, following the others over the crunch of feet on the path, I see even young people weeping, they put down their flowers and sometimes sheets of paper with what looks like lines of poems written there (I can't read this language well), and I see that the inquiry goes on, it will not end until they find the face, until the back of nobody turns about. And that will never happen. Now I do what the others do. It's the way to be safe, perfectly safe. Today I bought a cheap bunch of red roses held by an elastic band wound tight between their crushed leaves and wet thorns, and laid it there, before the engraved stone, behind the low railing, where my name is buried with him.

Further reading

You can listen to an excellent five-minute interview about Nadine Gordimer's life in South Africa and her experience of apartheid at http://www.bbc.co.uk/bbcfour/audiointerviews/profilepages/gordimer n1.shtml

Activities

The Hunting of Death

Before you read

1   Different cultures and religions have various beliefs about death and the afterlife. What do you believe about death? What do others in your class believe? Make your own notes and then share your ideas with the rest of your class.

What's it about?

Read the story and answer questions 2 to 4 by yourself. Then compare your answers with a partner's.

2   People often use myths to make sense of the natural world. Copy out six nouns from page 64 that establish the story's setting in the natural world. The first one is done for you: *nest*

3   How would you describe the character of Death in this story?

4   Is what happens in this story the woman's fault? Why / why not?

Thinking about the text

5   Explain in your own words how this Rwandan myth makes sense of death. Discuss the four points below with a partner and make some notes. Then write up your answer in four paragraphs. Use quotations to support your answer.

   ● Death is a natural process and this story is set in the natural world.
   ● God is both a caring and an aggressive figure.
   ● Humans are weak and easily overcome.
   ● Death is a clever and sly figure.

6   In this story, Death is made into a person. This is called personification (giving human qualities to objects or ideas). Pick one of the characteristics below and imagine you are its personification.

   greed   anger   laziness   jealousy

   Write a list of:
   ● what you would look like   ● where you might live
   ● what you might say   ● what you might do.

   Hot-seat some of the students in your class and try to find out which characteristics they personify. If you are in the hot seat, use your drama skills to convey the characteristic you have chosen.

Cassien's Story

Before you read

1   Many of the survivors of the Rwandan genocide were left without any family or possessions. Who are the most important people in your life? Which of your possessions do you treasure? Draw a spider diagram with yourself in the middle and the people and possessions you value most around the edge. Now think about how different your life would be without them. Discuss your ideas with the rest of your class.

What's it about?

Read the text and answer questions 2 to 4 by yourself. Then compare your answers with a partner's.

2   How did Cassien escape being killed three times?

3   Chronological reports often contain connectives related to time. Find three examples of this in Cassien's story. The first one is done for you: *immediately*

4   Cassien dropped out of school, but evidence in this text shows that he is an intelligent boy. Copy out the sentence that proves this.

Thinking about the text

5   Write your own autobiographical text on one of the following topics:
   ● A frightening experience
   ● A turning point in my life

   Whilst an horrific experience like Cassien's is unusual, you should try to convey the significance of the events of your own story by using descriptive language to help your reader picture the scene and how you felt.

6   '*Cassien's Story* is a shocking text that makes us reconsider our own childhood.' Write a short essay discussing how this text has affected you personally. Use the questions below to help you structure your writing:
   ● What did you know about Rwanda before you read this text?
   ● Have you learned anything new from reading this text?
   ● What did you learn about Cassien's character?
   ● Has this text changed your opinions about anything?
   ● How has this text made you reflect on your own life?

Snipers

Before you read

1   Some people make a strong impression on us when we are young. Think of someone you remember from your childhood. Write down five things you particularly remember about them.

2   What does the word 'snipers' mean? Look it up in a dictionary and discuss in a small group what associations the word has for you.

What's it about?

Read the poem and answer questions 3 to 5 by yourself. Then discuss your answers in a small group.

3   Uncle Tom's return from the war was celebrated by his family. In what traditional English way did they celebrate? Use quotations from the poem to support your answer.

4   Roger McGough uses a simile in verse two. Identify the simile and explain its effect on the reader.

5   Uncle Tom has been badly affected by the war.
   a   What clues in verses three and four show this?
   b   Look again at the final two lines of the poem. Who or what is Uncle Tom fighting now he is not fighting 'the Japs'?

Thinking about the text

6   Imagine that you are the young Roger McGough. Your Uncle Tom came home from Burma a few days ago. Write a short diary entry explaining your thoughts and feelings about your uncle. Use facts from the poem to help you.

7   How does the poem *Snipers* describe the effects of war on normal people? Write a short essay in answer to this question, using the plan below to structure your answer. Remember to comment on the language of the poem, using quotations to support your answers.

   ● Summary of what the poem is about
   ● Uncle Tom as a hero
   ● Uncle Tom as weak
   ● Conclusion: the important message in the last two lines of the poem

Cut Me, and I Bleed Khaki

Before you read

1   Look at the picture of the military man on page 88. Discuss the questions below with a partner.
   • What assumptions would you make about this person from what you can see? What words would you use to describe him?
   • What positive character traits would you guess he has?
   • What negative character traits would you guess he has?

What's it about?

Read the story and answer questions 2 to 4 by yourself. Then compare your answers with a partner's.

2   The beginning of the story starts after the events the writer is going to describe. At this point, what are the following people doing and what does it show about them? Copy and complete the table.

Character	What they are doing and what this shows about them
The narrator of the story, 'Skinny'	
Squadron Leader Major Bathurst	
Other soldiers	

3   What did Skinny feel he missed out on after his father's death?

4   Why does the writer use italics on page 86?

Thinking about the text

5   Consider Skinny's relationship with his father.
   a   Before Skinny was five, his father was affectionate towards him. Copy out two words or phrases from pages 75–76 that prove this.
   b   There was a turning point in his relationship with his father when he was five. What happened and why do you think it changed things?

6   Discuss the title of this story with a partner. What does it mean and how does it relate to the narrator's experience? Summarise your conclusions in a paragraph and then share them with the rest of your class.

Barefoot Gen

Before you read

1   Can you think of any comics or other popular text types that address serious issues for young people today? Discuss your answer with the rest of your class.

What's it about?

Read the story and write a sentence or two in answer to questions 2 and 3.

2   Read the story, then look again at page 90. How do the opening images and dialogue establish the mood and setting?

3   The pilot says 'Wow . . . it's like being in a tin can that's been hit with a **baseball bat!**' What does this simile suggest about the people dropping the bomb?

Thinking about the text

4   Write down five words that you think best summarise the effect of Hiroshima as described in this story. Discuss these with a partner and agree on a final five words to share with the rest of your class.

5   Find out about Hiroshima and the nuclear bomb. As well as using the Internet and the library, you could talk to members of your family, some of whom might remember it being dropped. Working in a small group, prepare a three-minute factual presentation using ten of the most interesting or important things you have found out about Hiroshima. End with your personal opinion about what happened. You may like to use presentation software such as Powerpoint with text and images to support what you say. You could start by using the free online encyclopaedia Wikipedia, or visit one of these websites:
   - http://www.pbs.org/wgbh/amex/truman/psources/ps_pressre lease.html
   - http://www.nuclearfiles.org/

Enola Gay

Before you read

1   What are the top ten characteristics you would put on a 'character shopping list' for a mother? Write your own list and then agree
a final list with a partner.

What's it about?

Read the poem and answer questions 2 and 3 by yourself. Then discuss your answers in a small group.

2   Here is what the poet tells us about her inspiration behind the
poem.

*I'd always been intrigued by the name 'Enola Gay' – it's such a pretty name
and yet it's associated with a horrifying event. Then when I found out that it
was actually the name of the flight captain's mother I knew I wanted to write
a poem about her. I wanted to present her as an ordinary woman, doing ordinary domestic tasks, to try and 'rescue' her from her association with the
atomic bomb.*

Morgan imagines Enola Gay as a very 'ordinary' woman. Copy out
any words and phrases in the poem that suggest this.

3   How does the word 'stainlessly' contrast with the actions of the
plane and her son? Write a short paragraph explaining your answer.

Thinking about the text

4   We usually associate stars with hope. Why do you think the
mother's dreams and the plane's flight are in a sky that is 'starless'?
Discuss your ideas with the rest of your class.

5   According to the poem, what might be the similarities and differences between Enola Gay the plane and Enola Gay the woman?

Homage

Before you read

1   The news headlines are often full of violent crimes. In some areas of this country, and in countries around the world, this is increasingly part of everyday life. In a small group, discuss what you know about the following crimes and why they are particularly memorable:

- the assassination of President Kennedy
- the murder of Damilola Taylor
- the September 11 attacks
- the Soham murders.

For what reasons might someone feel they have to commit such acts?

What's it about?

Read the story and answer questions 2 to 5 by yourself. Then compare your answers with a partner's.

2   Where is the narrator of this story sitting? Who is he talking to?

3   Why did he kill someone? Use quotations from the story to support your answer.

4   Copy out a sentence that shows this story is written in the first person. Why do you think the author has chosen to write this in the first person and how does that make you feel?

5   Why do you think the narrator of this story places roses by the gravestone of the person he murdered?

Thinking about the text

6   Why do you think the author chooses not to name the narrator?

7   Imagine that the murderer is to be interviewed by a probation officer, so that the officer can advise the court on an appropriate punishment. Working with a partner, write the script of the interview. Focus on the facts of the crime and the criminal's motivation. Practise the interview, then perform it for the rest of your class.

8   Find out more about the history of apartheid in South Africa and the role of Nelson Mandela in changing the political face of South Africa. Use the Internet and your school library. Write two paragraphs summarising the key points in your own words.

Compare and contrast

1 Many texts in this section convey human suffering. Compare and contrast the three texts *Barefoot Gen*, *Snipers* and *Cassien's Story*. Discuss:
   - the kind of human suffering described
   - whether it is fiction or non-fiction
   - how the writer conveys this experience to the reader through any of the following elements: language, structure, setting, characterisation, events
   - whether this is linked to the country the text is from and, if so, how.

   Copy and complete the table below to compare and contrast the texts *Enola Gay* and *Barefoot Gen* in their portrayal of the horror of Hiroshima. The first example is completed for you.

Similarity/difference	Enola Gay and Barefoot Gen
Similarity	The setting of 'Enola Gay' is domestic, describing the home and domestic chores of Enola Gay Tibbets, the mother of the commander of the plane that dropped the bomb on Hiroshima. The setting of 'Barefoot Gen' is also domestic in that it focuses on a family living in Hiroshima.
Difference	The setting of the poem is geographically distant from Japan as it is set in the home of Enola Gay in America, whereas 'Barefoot Gen' is set in Hiroshima where the direct effect of the bomb was experienced.

2 Many of the texts in this section are directly linked to events in their country of origin. Select two texts from this section and write a paragraph on what you have learned about the history or culture of the country from the text. You might like to consider one or more of the following: *characters setting language events*.

3 Much of this section focuses on human unhappiness and suffering. Which of the texts end on a more happy or hopeful note? In a small group, discuss the texts and their endings and note down which you think leave the reader with a positive feeling. Give reasons for your answers.

3 Personal freedom

Many people in Western society take personal freedom for granted, but in some countries around the world it is restricted. Freedom is about being physically free – being able to move around without imprisonment – and about being allowed to think, speak or write freely and to make personal lifestyle choices. This section focuses on what it is like to have one's freedom restricted. Some of the texts look at confinement, in prison or by war; others have been inspired by the experience of refugees – people who gain freedom from danger in one country, but feel trapped in another; others focus on the experience of children, restricted by the actions of adults and the society they live in.

Activities

1 Discuss with a partner the ways in which your personal freedom is limited by the law of your country.

   a List what you are not allowed to do as a minor (under 18) and when you are under 16. Decide which of the restrictions you think are fair and which you think are unfair. Choose one of each to share with the rest of your class during discussion.

   b Why does society think it is necessary to impose these rules on minors?

2 Discuss with a partner the ways in which your personal freedom is limited at home.

   a What rules do your parents or guardians impose on you? List which of these you think are fair and which you think are unfair, then compare your lists with your partner's.

   b Why do parents think it is necessary to impose such rules?

3 Imagine that Emily Lawrence, aged 15, is a girl in your class. She has made a list of the restrictions imposed on her at home and at school. Working with a partner, order them so that what you consider to be the most acceptable limitations on her freedom are at

the top, and the least acceptable at the bottom. Be prepared to justify your choices.

- Not allowed chips for school dinners more than once a week.
- Not allowed to make racist comments in school.
- Not allowed to go out on weekday evenings during termtime.
- Not allowed to have a Saturday job.
- Not allowed to leave school at 16 – my parents want me to do A levels.
- Not allowed to relax in the evenings – need to do homework instead.
- Not allowed to leave my bedroom after 8 o'clock in the evening.
- Not allowed to wear make-up in school.
- Not allowed to eat meat at home – my parents are vegetarian.
- Not allowed to have friends who are boys in my bedroom.
- Not allowed to go on holiday with my friends.

Zlata's Diary (Bosnia)

by Zlata Filipović

As a young girl, Zlata Filopović wrote a moving and informing diary about her life in Sarajevo during the siege of 1992, part of the Bosnian War. It begins just before her eleventh birthday in 1991 and ends just before they escaped to Paris in 1993. It chronicles her daily life and records the effect of war on the freedom and happiness of her family. As a result of the war, Zlata rarely had food, water or electricity, and lived in poverty and fear.

The introduction to *Zlata's Diary* was written by the journalist Krishnan Guru-Murthy in response to a visit he made to Zlata's home in Sarajevo in 1993. In it, Guru-Murthy highlights the impact war has had on Zlata's life.

After the introduction by Guru-Murthy you will find two extracts from *Zlata's Diary*. They are taken from the beginning and near the end of her diary, and show the contrast between her life before and during the war. *Zlata's Diary* was translated into English by Christina Pribichevich-Zorić.

Introduction

by Krishnan Guru-Murthy

Imagine waking up to the sound of gunfire and explosions. It's so loud it sounds like it's coming from the next room, it shakes your bed and it is terrifying. Then imagine turning on the light and everything staying dark because there's no electricity, walking to the bathroom to splash your face and finding there isn't any water in the taps. You walk to the kitchen to have your breakfast, except there isn't any food. Your mum is sitting with your dad and they both look scared. They say you cannot leave the house because it is too dangerous outside. Imagine all of that and then imagine it happening day after day after day.

Zlata Filipović didn't have to imagine all of that, because it really happened to her. It also happened to thousands of other children living in what was Yugoslavia. What makes Zlata's experiences special is the fact that we can try to share them, because she wrote them down in a small black diary.

I first met Zlata just before Christmas 1993 in her home in Sarajevo. I had heard about her diary and was there to make a television programme about it. She lived with her parents in a smart flat just by the river and across from a small park. I'm sure it was once a lovely place to live, but when I arrived it was very bleak. That part of the city was being bombed a great deal and the shops across the road were in ruins. There were no trees in the park – Zlata told me they had all been chopped up for firewood.

Zlata started her diary in November 1991 before the war began in Sarajevo. It was a place to write down what she thought about things. She called the diary 'Mimmy'. 'It's like having a friend who you can tell everything to,' she said. Her life before the war was a lot like that of other eleven-year-old girls. She enjoyed spending time with her friends, watching MTV, eating pizza and playing the piano. She enjoyed school and often went to a neighbour's house with her friends to have extra English lessons. Her mum worked in a chemical laboratory and her dad was a lawyer, so they were fairly well off. They even had a beautiful holiday home out in the country.

On Zlata's bedroom wall is a calendar. The date on it is frozen at 5 April 1992. That was the day Zlata's life was turned upside down. The war that had started over the break up of Yugoslavia spread to Sarajevo. When Zlata showed me the calendar she said, 'That was the day that time stood still. One day, when Sarajevo is back to normal, I'll start changing the date on the calendar again.'

Over the next few months of 1992 Zlata's life changed dramatically. Like all of her friends she didn't understand why there was a war. She hated being frightened during the bombing and having to run down to the cellar to take cover. She hated the boredom of having to stay inside all the time. And she hated being unable to escape. Throughout this time she wrote down her thoughts. On 7 May 1992 her friend Nina was killed in a bomb attack. 'Is it possible', she wrote, 'I'll never see Nina again . . . A disgusting war has destroyed a young child's life. Nina, I'll always remember you as a wonderful little girl.'

Zlata never dreamed that her diary would become her passport to freedom. But at the end of 1993 a French company decided to publish the diary. With some help from the French government and the United Nations troops who were trying to bring peace, Zlata and her family were flown to Paris.

Zlata is now safe, but her thoughts remain with the thousands of children like her who are still trapped by the fighting. Since leaving Sarajevo she has travelled far and wide telling people about her experiences, and her diary is being read all over the world. She will never forget what happened or the need to stop what is still going on. Thanks to her writing, perhaps we will be reminded too.

Krishnan Guru-Murthy
Newsround, BBC, 1994

The BBC's *Newsround* programme went to Sarajevo on 14 December 1993 to make a documentary about Zlata and her diary, the week before Zlata and her family finally left.

Zlata's Diary
by Zlata Filipović

Monday, 2 September 1991

Behind me – a long, hot summer and the happy days of summer holidays; ahead of me – a new school year. I'm starting fifth grade. I'm looking forward to seeing my friends at school, to being together again. Some of them I haven't seen since the day the school bell rang, marking the end of term. I'm glad we'll be together again, and share all the worries and joys of going to school.

Mirna, Bojana, Marijana, Ivana, Maša, Azra, Minela, Nadža – we're all together again.

Tuesday, 10 September 1991

The week was spent getting my books and school supplies, describing how we spent our holidays on the seaside, in the mountains, in the countryside and abroad. We all went somewhere and we all have so much to tell one another.

Thursday, 19 September 1991

Classes have also started at music school now. I go twice a week for piano and solfeggio. I'm continuing my tennis lessons. Oh yes, I've been moved up to the 'older' group in tennis. Wednesdays I go to Auntie Mika's for English lessons. Tuesdays I have choir practice. Those are my responsibilities. I have six lessons every day, except Fridays. I'll survive . . .

Monday, 23 September 1991

I don't know if I mentioned my workshop class (it's a new subject) which starts in fifth grade. Our teacher is Jasmina Turajlić and I LIKE HER. We learn about wood, what it is, how it's used, and it's pretty interesting. Soon we'll be moving on to practical work, which means making various things out of wood and other materials. It'll be interesting.

The teachers have already started testing us, there's history, geography, biology. I have to study!

Friday, 27 September 1991

I'm home from school and I'm really tired. It's been a hard week. Tomorrow is Saturday and I can sleep as long as I like. LONG LIVE SATURDAYS! Tomorrow night, I'm 'busy'. Tomorrow is Ivana Varunek's birthday party. I received an invitation today. More about this next time . . .

Sunday, 29 September 1991

It's now 11.00 a.m. Ivana's birthday is actually today but she had her party yesterday. It was super. There were little rolls, things to munch on, sandwiches and, most important of all – a cake. Boys were invited as well as girls. We had a dance contest and I won. My prize was a little 'jewellery' box. All in all it was a great party.

Sunday, 6 October 1991

I'm watching the American Top 20 on MTV. I don't remember a thing, who's in what place.

I feel great because I've just eaten a 'Four Seasons' PIZZA with ham, cheese, ketchup and mushrooms. It was yummy. Daddy bought it for me at Galija's (the pizzeria around the corner). Maybe that's why I didn't remember who took what place – I was too busy enjoying my pizza.

I've finished studying and tomorrow I can go to school BRAVELY, without being afraid of getting a bad grade. I deserve a good grade because I studied all weekend and I didn't even go out to play with my friends in the park. The weather is nice and we usually play 'monkey in the middle', talk and go for walks. Basically, we have fun.

Sunday, 2 May 1993

Dear Mimmy,

Do you remember 2 May 1992, the worst day in this misery of a life? I often say that maybe it wasn't the most awful day, but it was the first of the most awful days, and so I think of it as the worst. I'll never forget the stench of the cellar, the hunger, the shattering glass, the horrible shelling. We went for twelve hours without food or water, but the worst thing was the fear, huddling in the corner of the cellar, and the uncertainty of what was going to happen. Not understanding what was happening. It gives me the shivers just to think about it.

It's been a year since then, a year in which every day has been 2 May. But here I am still alive and healthy, my family is alive and well, sometimes we have electricity, water and gas and we get the odd scrap of food. KEEP GOING. But for how long, does anyone really know?

Zlata

Monday, 3 May 1993

Dear Mimmy,

Auntie Boda and Žika got letters from Bojana and Maja today. They're okay, they eat, drink, worry . . .

Apart from the letters, we leafed through the Bosnian language dictionary. I don't know what to say, Mimmy. Perhaps – too many 'h's, which until now was looked on as a spelling mistake. What's to be done????

It's been a long time since I wrote to you about what I've been reading. Well, let me tell you now: *Famous Seafarers, Three Hearts, The Spark of Life, The Jottings of an Ana, Bare Face, The Wrath of the Angels, The Famous Five, A Man, a Woman and a Child, Territorial Rights, Somebody Else's Little Girl, I Was a Drug Addict, Delusion* and . . . and I also often leaf through the photographs in cookbooks, it makes me feel as though I've eaten what I'm looking at.

Zlata

Tuesday, 4 May 1993

Dear Mimmy,

I've been thinking about politics again. No matter how stupid, ugly and unreasonable I think this division of people into Serbs, Croats and Muslims is, these stupid politics are making it happen. We're all waiting for something, hoping for something, but there's nothing. Even the Vance–Owen peace plan looks as though it's going to fall through. Now these maps are being drawn up, separating people, and nobody asks them a thing. Those 'kids' really are playing around with us. Ordinary people don't want this division, because it won't make anybody happy – not the Serbs, not the Croats, not the Muslims. But who asks ordinary people? Politics asks only its own people.

Your Zlata

Further reading

Other books that draw on the experience of refugees include *The People of Sparks* by Jeanne DuPrau (Corgi Children's, 2006), *Divided City* by Theresa Breslin (Corgi Children's, 2006), *Kiss the Dust* by Elizabeth Laird (Macmillan Children's Books, 2007) and *Little Soldier* by Bernard Ashley (Scholastic, 2002).

Cruelty to Children (India)

by R. K. Narayan

Narayan is generally recognised as one of the first significant Indian authors to write about India in the English language. This is the speech that he delivered to the Indian Parliament when he was elected because of his cultural contribution to the country. He used this chance to highlight society's responsibility for children. Like many of his short stories, this piece uses gentle humour to make his audience think about an important issue – what should childhood be about and how does government policy affect this?

This speech focuses on the experience of a schoolchild. Narayan himself spent part of his working life as an English teacher. As a child he did not enjoy school: his first school was a Mission school where Hindus like him were not treated kindly, and his second school was run by his father, who was the headmaster.

In the stress of the concerns of the adult world, the problems or rather the plight[1] of children pass unnoticed. I am not referring to any particular class but to childhood itself. The hardship starts right at home, when straight from sleep the child is pulled out and got ready for school even before its faculties[2] are awake. He (or she) is groomed and stuffed into a uniform and packed off to school with a loaded bag on his back. The school-bag has become an inevitable[3] burden for the child. I am now pleading for abolition[4] of the school-bag, as a national policy, by an ordinance[5] if necessary. I have investigated and found that an average child carries strapped to his back, like a pack-mule, not less than six to eight kgs of books, notebooks and other paraphernalia[6] of modern education in addition to lunch-box and water bottle. Most

[1]**plight**   unpleasant condition
[2]**faculties**   the natural ability to see, hear, think, move etc.
[3]**inevitable**   unavoidable
[4]**abolition**   banning
[5]**ordinance**   law made by government
[6]**paraphernalia**   objects connected with a particular activity

children on account of this daily burden develop a stoop and hang their arms forward like a chimpanzee while walking, and I know cases of serious spinal injuries in some children too. Asked why not leave some books behind at home, the child explains it is her teacher's orders that all books and notes must be brought every day to the class, for what reason God alone knows. If there is a lapse, the child invites punishment, which takes the form of being rapped on the knuckles with a wooden scale, a refinement from our days when we received cane cuts on the palm only. The child is in such terror of the teacher, whether known as Sister, Mother Superior, or just Madam, that he or she is prepared to carry out any command issued by the teacher, who has no imagination or sympathy.

The dress regulation particularly in convent schools is another senseless formality – tie and laced shoes and socks, irrespective of[7] the climate, is compulsory.[8] Polishing a shoe and lacing it becomes a major task for a child first thing in the day. When the tie has become an anachronism[9] even in the adult world, it's absurd to enforce it on children. A simple uniform and footwear must be designed and brought into force and these should be easier to maintain.

After school hours when the child returns home her mother or home tutor is waiting to pounce on her, snatch her bag and compel[10] her to go through some special coaching or homework. For the child the day has ended; with no time left for her to play or dream. It is a cruel, harsh life imposed on her, and I present her case before this house for the honourable members to think out and devise remedies by changing the whole educational system and outlook so that childhood has a chance to bloom rather than wilt in the process of learning.

Other areas where the child needs protection is from involvement in adult activities such as protest marches,

---

[7]**irrespective of**   without considering
[8]**compulsory**   required, obligatory
[9]**anachronism**   something that is outside its correct time in history
[10]**compel**   force

parades, or lining up on road-sides for waving in VIPs; children are made to stand in the hot sun for hours without anyone noticing how much they suffer from fatigue, hunger and thirst. Children must be protected, and cherished, which would seem especially relevant in this year of the Nehru centenary. How it is to be done is upto our rulers and administrators to consider – perhaps not by appointing a commission of enquiry, but in some other practical and peaceful manner.

Further reading

R. K. Narayan is particularly well known for his short stories. For a challenging read, try the collection *Malgudi Days* (Penguin, 2006) or *Under the Banyan Tree* (Penguin, 2001). For more recent stories that often focus on Indian/British experience, try the writing of Jamila Gavin or Farrukh Dhondy.

Guess Who Is Coming to Dinner (Bosnia)

by Darija Stojnić

> This short story was written by a Bosnian writer who entered the UK as a refugee as a result of the siege of Sarajevo in 1992. Unlike *Zlata's Diary*, which focuses on the immediate effects of war and poverty, this story focuses on the challenges and hardships of moving to another country as a refugee and how refugees are treated by others.

Rich middle-class English housewives are so easily recognisable. They are in perfect shape, dress mainly in expensive trousers and flat golden shoes, have perfect hair, lightly tanned faces and beautiful nails. They smell expensive, are always polite and smiling, but are incredibly arrogant – a way to rid themselves of their working class origins, I dare to suggest. They do not know what to do with their surplus energy and time. They work steadily more on appearance than on education.

Having refugees for dinner is almost prestigious[1] in the circle of these bored, rich, superficial women. I was delighted to have been invited to one such home. How naive of me.

'Sit, please,' my hostess shouted, tapping the seat where she expected me to sit.

'Thank you very much,' I replied

'Oh, you speak English,' she put on her best smile, as if she was delighted with the discovery.

'A little,' I answered politely.

'Your Russian must be very good.'

'Why should I speak Russian?' I dared to ask back, and a brief thought went through my mind: 'Oh, help me Lord. I do not have any chance with her.'

---

[1] **prestigious**   greatly respected and admired, usually because of being important

'My dear, what was your name?' she asked reassuringly. 'As far as I know, all communist[2] countries were under Russia. Am I right?'

'I am so sorry, but we were an independent country. We did not belong to any Eastern or Western bloc, we were . . . '

'O, my dear,' she interrupted me. 'We know everything about your country and this dreadful war you have in Czechoslovakia, where you've come from. Don't worry, you are safe now in England.'

'Yes, but . . . not Czech . . . ' I tried. And again: 'Not Czechoslovakia.' I wanted to say: 'I came from former Yugoslavia,' but I did not have a chance.

'Have you ever been abroad?' she asked me, with the most emphatic[3] facial expression you can imagine. 'London must be a wonderful new experience,' she went on.

'I used to travel a lot, and I spent nearly six months in the south-east of England, and in London of course.' I replied.

'Oh, did you?' She lost her plot. The disappointed silence was broken by an announcement that dinner was ready.

I entered the most beautiful dinning room I have ever seen. Everything was perfect, from the stunning interior to the crockery, cutlery, the glasses on the table, and of course the remarkable guests. All of them rich, with a perfect image, chatty, full of self-confidence.

I was the only one who was not perfect. I was heartbroken, financially broken, dressed from a charity shop, feeling so uncomfortable, wanting to run away. But how could I? I was a special guest, although I felt more like the main course, invited for dinner as a great honour to show me – and to prove to each other – how much they cared about me. Did they?

My hostess touched me gently and whispered in my ear:

'Are you OK with a knife and fork?' The waves of humiliation swept through me like a thunderstorm, but I managed to

---

[2]**communist**   a society ruled by the belief that there are no different classes, in which the methods of production are owned and controlled by all its members and everyone works as much as they can and receives what they need
[3]**emphatic**   strong

use my last vestiges[4] of wit and whispered back: 'I'll try not to cut myself.'

After this I had enough. I just wanted to faint and lie unconscious on the floor until everything was over. But I was not that lucky. I had to remain fully conscious all the way through dinner.

'Did you go to school down there?'

'Yes, I am a lawyer,' I simply said.

'Oh, really?' Then a pause, to deliver a big thought. 'Of course, you can be a lawyer here. Can't you?'

'No, I cannot because my English will never be good enough and the British Law Society does demand . . . '

'Nonsense, dear. Your English is much better than my Croatian,[5] or whatever the name of it is. But if you do not want to be a lawyer, you can always be a nurse. Isn't that a good idea, my dear?' I gathered my strength in a desperate attempt not to say anything.

'Thank you for having me,' I said to my hostess on my way out.

'It was a pleasure,' she replied, then kissed me goodbye.

I have never ever been invited again.

Thank God.

Further reading

A powerful and popular book about the refugee experience in England is *Refugee Boy* by Benjamin Zephaniah (Bloomsbury, 2001).

---

[4]**vestige**   a still existing small part of something larger
[5]**Croatian**   the language of Croatia

The Mailed Parcel (Iraq)

by Ibrahim Ahmed

This story of a refugee couple focuses on the topic of letter bombs. These have been used extensively across the world by terrorists who wish to harm or frighten the employees of a particular organisation or, less frequently, specific individuals. They are generally associated with political intimidation and protest. This specific issue is used by the author to highlight the continuing distress that refugees face, even once they are 'safe' in another country. This story was translated into English by Lily Al-Tai.

On that day they did not have any lessons at the language school. They were busy with the domestic chores when the mail-flap clicked. He remarked to his wife that this time they might have dropped through some coupons for flour, and quickly went to find out.

On top of the usual colourful papers he found a dark-coloured parcel. He examined it calmly. He thought it must have been delivered to him by mistake, but discovered that it was addressed to him in vague handwriting as if the sender was not entirely certain of his address. But where had the sender obtained his address from? He remembered, in the camps, he had exchanged addresses with Iraqi refugees, to keep in touch in the course of their long path ahead.

He was about to open it eagerly, but his fingers hesitated at the edges of the parcel; he was suddenly overwhelmed with fear. It occurred to him it might be a parcel bomb. He remembered what he had seen on television a few days ago about an explosion in which a Kurdish woman and her daughter had both been killed by a parcel bomb. What exacerbated[1] his unease, was the fact that the parcel was from abroad with Czech stamps on it and no name of the sender only postmarks and some

---

[1]**exacerbate**   to make worse something that was already bad

deletions and scribbles added. So this parcel had been on his trail throughout his wanderings through the camps. It might have been sent to his first address in Sweden. He thought it unlikely for a parcel bomb to pass through all those places undetected. His wife came up to him, prompting him and inquiring:

'What is this?' but he quickly signalled to her cautiously when she was about to pick it up. He distanced her from it saying:

'It might be booby-trapped.' She carried on looking at him disconcertedly and said:

'Who are we, for them to send us a parcel bomb?'

He had stopped his political work after they had had a child. When he worked in politics, he had been neither a leader nor a prominent figure. He said:

'And what were the Kurdish woman and her daughter up to when they murdered them with a parcel bomb?' The wife said:

'We have been forsaken[2] to the end of the world.' He said, staring at the parcel:

'Sometimes they murder people of lesser significance than ourselves to frighten others!'

He carefully placed the parcel in an empty corner by the door.

For a long time now, they had stopped expecting mail. In Algeria, almost a year after leaving Iraq, their first and only son had drowned at the seaside when they were on an outing. The shock had almost crushed them both. They were frightened of informing their families in Iraq who were attached to the child for, when they were leaving, they had asked to keep the child. A cryptic[3] letter had arrived from their families requesting that they did not correspond with them; but they understood. Their families, like others, received their mail from the party headquarters and security bureaus of their districts. Yet they still feared receiving a letter from the family asking about the child.

Their letters to friends abroad were spasmodic and reluctant and had now stopped for they carried no news other than

[2]**forsaken**   left or abandoned, especially by people you need
[3]**cryptic**   mysterious and difficult to understand

catastrophes, tragedies and misfortunes which they could no longer bear to hear about. They now feared the postman and were scared when he appeared, repeating to each other that they 'could no longer handle a letter'.

They had had two children in the course of their migration[4] to various countries. They had arrived in Sweden not more than a year ago, anguished by exile.[5] Their savings had dwindled. They had been transported to various refugee camps and were sent to live in a small town by the sea.

In the first week of their arrival, they received a letter with a plastic green key from one of the supermarkets inviting them to collect two hundred and fifty grams of coffee, as a token of hospitality and welcome. It was a successful commercial and humane[6] gesture.

The man held the letter fearlessly, remarking to his wife that no longer was coffee the Arab symbol of hospitality and magnanimity.[7] In the many Arab countries in which they had found themselves, they had been received with annoyance, dejection and meanness. In Algeria, when their child had drowned, the father's spirit and health had been destroyed, and yet they did not renew his teaching contract but asked him instead to vacate the house and country within weeks.

Here they had found security, peace and a carefree life marred only when they saw in each other's eyes, the waves of the sea in the darkness of the nights carrying them to the vortex[8] of that distant past and its devastating nightmares awakening in their hearts the vision of that beautiful child drowning and fading in front on their eyes in the nearby deeps of the sea, while they both stood helplessly looking on.

---

[4]**migration**   movement from one place to another to live

[5]**exile**   the condition of being sent or kept away from your own country for political reasons

[6]**humane**   showing kindness to others, especially those who are suffering

[7]**magnanimity**   kindness and generosity to a defeated enemy or someone less important

[8]**vortex**   mass of spinning air or water pulling air or water into its empty space

They busied themselves learning the Swedish language in preparation for work.

Everyday when the man heard the click of the mail-flap, his heart would throb; getting to the front door was like reaching a haunted place at night. But as he often found magazines, supermarket adverts and colourful fliers with attractive offers for food, clothes, cars and castles, mingled every so often with one or two letters from friends or the local authorities, he shook his head and laughed, remarking to his wife:

'Perhaps all the junk mail has had one benefit. It has enabled us to hold a letter again.'

Up to now, they had found opening letters in this part of the world an experience that was not frightening. It no longer seemed to them, as it once had, like the opening of a grave. They now felt able to receive letters from their families and to reply to their questions. They did not, however, dwell too much on such hopes since their families had heard nothing from them for some years now. They too did not know what had become of them, or whether their address had changed since the Authorities and the Party still regulated everything.

The man was happy to hear the clicking sound of the metal mail-flap. It sounded like the rustling of two heavy twigs dropping their ripe fruits on the ground. The pictures of commodities and the advertisements with their bright colours and prices consoled him as it made him feel that there existed a world immersed in benevolence[9] and pleasure, not catastrophe.

But this parcel in the corner seems to him now something else. He approached it imagining that it might explode in the faces of his two children on their return from school. His wife told him to place it on the balcony, but changed her mind when she remembered that it was covered in snow. The man became irritated and said:

'Shall we call the police?' The wife was in a calmer state and replied:

---

[9]**benevolence**   kindness

'We will show it to the postman.'

But the man thought it horrifying to spend the night with a bomb in the house. The wife sensed this through his anxious glances and unrest and said she wanted to go shopping and that he could accompany her to the post office which was on the way. He decided to risk carrying the parcel. As he walked on the snow, the chill winds penetrating, he feared he might slip and that the parcel would land on him. So he walked slowly, careful not to shake the parcel or collide with one of the pedestrians on the snowy, narrow pavements. He kept a reasonable distance from his wife thinking that at least she should survive for the sake of the two children. With the hand carrying the parcel stretched away from his body, he persuaded himself that the explosion might sever his hand, which would be a reasonable sacrifice, but would not affect the rest of his body.

At the post office, in a mixture of English and Swedish, they spoke to a beautiful girl who sought the advice of one of the officers inside who carefully checked the parcel and said confidently:

'It is perfectly normal and safe.' When he saw they were both still apprehensive and looking at him in despair and sadness, he said to them: 'Do you wish me to open it?' The man nodded his head hastily. The officer opened the parcel and passed it to the man. The man removed the contents of the parcel and found a letter:

I could find no resting place. I have moved about a great deal. I am now clearing everything to prepare to emigrate to Australia. I did not wish to lose your precious belongings. I am certain that both of you with your two beautiful children look upon the past with strength and courage.

He opened another old and faded envelope. He found between his now trembling hands a picture of their drowned child and a lock of his hair. The Swedish officer could not understand why this man uttered a loud moan and why the woman broke down in tears. He began to look at them and at this place in which calm and order reigned, as if something had exploded which he had not heard.

Further reading

Other books for young people that draw on the experience of refugees include *The People of Sparks* by Jeanne DuPrau (Corgi Children's, 2006), *Divided City* by Theresa Breslin (Corgi Children's, 2006), *Kiss the Dust* by Elizabeth Laird (Macmillan Children's Books, 2007) and *Little Soldier* by Bernard Ashley (Scholastic, 2002).

Power (South Africa)

by Jack Cope

> There are several stories in this collection that draw on the political history of South Africa, where apartheid forced the people of South Africa to live apart as Blacks, Whites, Indians and 'Coloureds' for nearly fifty years. Under the regime, people's personal freedom was limited – they could not express themselves freely, movement was restricted and even a friendship with the 'wrong' person was dangerous. This South African story focuses on the crucial issues of freedom, using a simple story about a boy and a bird to reflect on the wider political issues of South Africa.

From the gum tree at the corner he looked out over, well – nothing. There was nothing more after his father's place, only the veld,[1] so flat and unchanging that the single shadowy koppie[2] away off towards the skyline made it look more empty still. It was a lonely koppie like himself.

The one thing that made a difference was the powerline. High above the earth on its giant steel lattice towers, the powerline strode across the veld until it disappeared beyond the koppie. It passed close to his father's place and one of the great pylons was on their ground in a square patch fenced off with barbed wire, a forbidden place. André used to look through the wire at the pylon. Around the steelwork itself were more screens of barbed wire, and on all four sides of it enamel warning-plates with a red skull-and-crossbones said in three languages, DANGER! And there was a huge figure of volts, millions of volts.

André was ten and he knew volts were electricity and the line took power by a short cut far across country. It worked gold mines, it lit towns, and hauled trains and drove machinery somewhere out beyond. The power station was in the town ten

---

[1]**veld**   flat open country with few trees, which is characteristic of parts of southern Africa

[2]**koppie**   a small hill rising up from the flat countryside

miles on the other side of his father's place and the great line simply jumped right over them without stopping.

André filled the empty spaces in his life by imagining things. Often he was a jet plane and roared around the house and along the paths with his arms outspread. He saw an Everest film once and for a long time he was Hillary or Tensing, or both, conquering a mountain. There were no mountains so he conquered the roof of the house which wasn't very high and was made of red-painted tin. But he reached the summit and planted a flag on the lightning conductor. When he got down his mother hit his legs with a quince switch for being naughty.

Another time he conquered the koppie. It took him the whole afternoon to get there and back and it was not as exciting as he expected, being less steep than it looked from a distance, so he did not need his rope and pick. Also, he found a cow had beaten him to the summit.

He thought of conquering one of the powerline towers. It had everything, the danger especially, and studying it from all sides he guessed he could make the summit without touching a live wire. But he was not as disobedient as all that, and he knew if he so much as went inside the barbed-wire fence his mother would skin him with the quince, not to mention his father. There were peaks which had to remain unconquered.

He used to lie and listen to the marvellous hum of the powerline, the millions of volts flowing invisible and beyond all one's ideas along the copper wires that hung so smooth and light from ties of crinkled white china looking like chinese lanterns up against the sky. Faint cracklings and murmurs and rushes of sound would sometimes come from the powerline, and at night he was sure he saw soft blue flames lapping and trembling on the wires as if they were only half peeping out of that fierce river of volts. The flames danced and their voices chattered to him of a mystery.

In the early morning when the mist was rising and the first sun's rays were shooting underneath it, the powerline sparkled like a tremendous spiderweb. It took his thoughts away into a magical distance, far – far off among gigantic machines and busy factories. That was where the world opened up. So he loved the powerline dearly. It made a door through the distance for his thoughts. It was like him except that it never slept, and while he was dreaming it went on without stopping, crackling faintly and murmuring. Its electricity hauled up the mine skips from the heart of the earth, hurtled huge green rail units along their shining lines, and thundered day and night in the factories.

Now that the veld's green was darkening and gathering black-and-gold tints from the ripe seeds and withering grass blades, now that clear warm autumn days were coming after the summer thunderstorms, the birds began gathering on the powerline. At evening he would see the wires like necklaces of blue-and-black glass beads when the swallows gathered. It took them days and days, it seemed, to make up their minds. He did not know whether the same swallows collected each evening in growing numbers or whether a batch went off each day to be replaced by others. He did not know enough about them. He loved to hear them making excited twittering sounds, he loved to see how they simply fell off the copper wire into space and their perfect curved wings lifted them on the air.

They were going not merely beyond the skyline like the power, they were flying thousands of miles over land and sea and mountains and forests to countries he had never dreamt of. They would fly over Everest, perhaps, they would see ships below them on blue seas among islands, they would build nests under bridges and on chimneys where other boys in funny clothes would watch them. The birds opened another door for him and he liked them too, very much.

He watched the swallows one morning as they took off from their perch. Suddenly, as if they had a secret signal, a whole stretch of them along a wire would start together. They dropped forward into the air and their blue-and-white wings flicked out. Flying seemed to be the easiest thing in the world. They swooped and flew up, crisscrossing in flight and chirping crazily, so pleased to be awake in the morning. Then another flight of them winged off, and another. There was standing-room only on those wires. Close to the lofty pylon and the gleaming china ties another flight took off. But one of the swallows stayed behind, quite close to the tie. André watched them fall forward, but it alone did not leave the line. It flapped its wings and he saw it was caught by its leg.

He should have been going to school but he stood watching the swallow, his cap pulled over his white hair and eyes wrinkled against the light. After a minute the swallow stopped flapping and hung there. He wondered how it could have got caught, maybe in the wire binding or at a join. Swallows had short legs and small black claws; he had caught one once in its nest and held it in his hands before it struggled free and was gone in a flash. He thought the bird on the powerline would get free soon, but looking at it there he had a tingling kind of pain in his chest and in one leg as if he too were caught by the foot. André wanted to rush back and tell his mother, only she would scold him for being late to school. So he climbed on his bike, and with one more look up at the helpless bird there against the sky and the steel framework of the tower, he rode off to the bus.

At school he thought once or twice about the swallow, but mostly he forgot about it and that made him feel bad. Anyway, he thought, it would be free by the time he got home. Twisting and flapping a few times, it was sure to work its foot out; and there was no need for him to worry about it hanging there.

Coming back from the crossroads he felt anxious, but he did not like to look up until he was quite near. Then he shot one glance at the top of the pylon – the swallow was still there, its wings spread but not moving. It was dead, he guessed, as he stopped and put down one foot. Then he saw it flutter and fold up its wings. He felt awful to think it had hung there all day, trapped. The boy went in and called his mother and they stood off some distance below the powerline and looked at the bird. The mother shaded her eyes with her hand. It was a pity, she said, but really she was sure it would free itself somehow. Nothing could be done about it.

'Couldn't – ?' he began.

'Couldn't nothing, dear,' she said quite firmly so that he knew she meant business. 'Now stop thinking about it, and tomorrow you'll see.'

His father came home at six and had tea, and afterwards there was a little time to work in his patch of vegetables out at the back. André followed him and he soon got round to the swallow on the powerline.

'I know,' his father said. 'Mama told me.'

'It's still there.'

'Well – ' his father tilted up his old working-hat and looked at him hard with his sharp blue eyes ' – well, we can't do anything about it, can we, now?'

'No, Papa, but – '

'But what?'

He kicked at a stone and said nothing more. He could see his father was kind of stiff about it; that meant he did not want to hear anything more. They had been talking about it, and maybe – yes, that was it. They were afraid he would try to climb up the pylon.

At supper none of them talked about the swallow, but André felt it all right. He felt as if it was hanging above their heads and his mother and father felt it and they all had a load on them. Going to bed his mother said to him he must not worry himself about the poor bird. 'Not a sparrow falls without our Good Lord knowing.'

'It's not a sparrow, it's a swallow,' he said. 'It's going to hang there all night, by its foot.' His mother sighed and put out the light. She was worried.

The next day was a Saturday and he did not have to go to school. First thing he looked out and the bird was still there. The other swallows were with it, and when they took off it fluttered and made little thin calls but could not get free.

He would rather have been at school instead of knowing all day that it was hanging up there on the cruel wire. It was strange how the electricity did nothing to it. He knew, of course, that the wires were quite safe as long as you did not touch anything else. The morning was very long, though he did forget about the swallow quite often. He was building a mud fort under the gum tree, and he had to carry water and dig up the red earth and mix it into a stiff clay. When he was coming in at midday with his khaki[3] hat flapping round his face he had one more look, and what he saw kept him standing there a long time with his mouth open. Other swallows were fluttering and hovering around the trapped bird, trying to help it. He rushed inside and dragged his mother out by her hand and she stood too, shading her eyes again and looking up.

---

[3]**khaki**   a dull yellowish-brown colour, often used for military clothing

'Yes, they're feeding it. Isn't that strange,' she said.

'Sssh! Don't frighten them,' he whispered.

In the afternoon he lay in the grass and twice again he saw the other swallows fluttering round the fastened bird with short quivering strokes of their wings and opening their beaks wide. Swallows had pouches in their throats where they made small mud bricks to build their nests, and that was how they brought food to it. They knew how to feed their fledglings and when the trapped bird squeaked and cried out they brought it food. André felt choked thinking how they helped it and nobody else would do anything. His parents would not even talk about it.

With his keen eyes he traced the way a climber could get up the tower. Most difficult would be to get round the barbed-wire screens about a quarter of the way up. After that there were footholds in the steel lattice supports. He had studied it before. But if you did get up, what then? How could you touch the swallow? Just putting your hand near the wire, wouldn't those millions of volts flame out and jump at you? The only thing was to get somebody to turn off the power for a minute, then he could whip up the tower like a monkey. At supper that night he suggested it, and his father was as grim and angry as he'd ever been.

'Crumbs,' André said to himself. 'Crumbs! They are both het up about it.'

'Listen, son,' his father had said. He never said 'son' unless he was really mad over something. 'Listen, I don't want you to get all worked up about that bird. I'll see what can be done. But you leave it alone. Don't get any ideas into your head, and don't go near that damned pylon.'

'What ideas, Papa?' he asked, trembling inside himself.

'Any ideas at all.'

'The other birds are feeding it, but it may die.'

'Well, I'm sorry; try not to think about it.'

When his mother came to say goodnight to him he turned his face over into his pillow and would not kiss her. It was something he had never done before and it was because he was angry with them both. They let the swallow swing there in the night and did nothing.

His mother patted his back and ruffled his white hair and said, 'Goodnight, darling.' But he gritted his teeth and did not answer.

Ages seemed to him to have passed. On Sunday the bird was still hanging on the lofty powerline, fluttering feebly. He could not bear to look up at it. After breakfast he went out and tried to carry on building his fort under the gum tree. The birds were chattering in the tree above him and in the wattles at the back of the house. Through the corner of his eye he saw a handsome black-and-white bird fly out in swinging loops from the tree and it settled on the powerline some distance from the tower. It was a butcher-bird, a Jackey-hangman, a terrible greedy pirate of a bird. His heart fell like a stone – he just guessed what it was up to. It sat there on the wire impudently copying the calls of other birds. It could imitate a toppie or a robin or a finch as it liked. It stole their naked little kickers from their nests and spiked them on the barbed wire to eat at pleasure, as it stole their songs too. The butcher-bird flew off and settled higher up the wire near the pylon.

André rushed up the path and then took a swing from the house to come under the powerline. Stopping, he saw the other birds were making a whirl and flutter round the cannibal. Swallows darted and skimmed and made him duck his head, but he went on sitting there. Then some starlings came screaming out of the gum tree and flew in a menacing bunch at the butcher-bird. They all hated him. He made the mistake of losing his balance and fluttered out into the air and all the birds were round him at once, darting and pecking and screaming.

The butcher-bird pulled off one of his typical tricks: he fell plumb down and when near the ground spread his wings, sailed low over the shrubs, and came up at the house where he settled on the lightning conductor. André stood panting and felt his heart beating fast. He wanted to throw a stone at the butcher-bird but he reckoned the stone would land on the roof and get him in trouble. So he ran towards the house waving his arms and shouting. The bird cocked its head and watched him.

His mother came out. 'Darling, what's the matter?'

'That Jackey, he's on the roof. He wanted to kill the swallow.'

'Oh, darling!' the mother said softly.

It was Sunday night and he said to his mother, 'It's only the other birds keeping him alive. They were feeding him again today.'

'I saw them.'

'He can't live much longer, Mama. And now the Jackey knows he's there. Why can't Papa get them to switch off the electricity?'

'They wouldn't do it for a bird, darling. Now try and go to sleep.'

Leaving for school on Monday, he tried not to look up. But he couldn't help it and there was the swallow spreading and closing its wings. He quickly got on his bike and rode as fast as he could. He could not think of anything but the trapped bird on the powerline.

After school, André did not catch the bus home. Instead he took a bus the other way, into town. He got out in a busy street and threading down through the factory area he kept his bearings on the four huge smokestacks of the power station. Out of two of the smokestacks white plumes[4] were rising calmly into the clear sky. When he got to the power station he was faced with an enormous high fence of iron staves with spiked tops and a tall steel gate, locked fast. He peered through the gate and saw some black men off duty, sitting in the sun on upturned boxes playing some kind of draughts game. He called them, and a big slow-moving man in brown overalls and a wide leather belt came over to talk.

André explained very carefully what he wanted. If they would switch off the current then he or somebody good at

---

[4]**plumes**   tall clouds of steam or smoke that look like large showy feathers

climbing could go up and save the swallow. The man smiled broadly and clicked his tongue. He shouted something at the others and they laughed. His name, he said, was Gas – Gas Makabeni. He was just a maintenance boy and he couldn't switch off the current. But he unlocked a steel frame-door in the gate and let André in.

'Ask them in there,' he said, grinning. André liked Gas very much. He had ESCOM in big cloth letters on his back and he was friendly, opening the door like that. André went with Gas through a high arched entrance and at once he seemed to be surrounded with the vast awesome hum of the power station. It made him feel jumpy. Gas took him to a door and pushed him in. A white engineer in overalls questioned him and he smiled too.

'Well,' he said. 'Let's see what can be done.'

He led him down a long corridor and up a short cut of steel zigzag steps. Another corridor came to an enormous panelled hall with banks of dials and glowing lights and men in long white coats sitting in raised chairs or moving about silently. André's heart was pounding good and fast. He could hear the humming sound strongly and it seemed to come from everywhere, not so much a sound as a feeling under his feet.

The engineer in overalls handed him over to one of the men at the control panels and he was so nervous by this time he took a long while trying to explain about the swallow. The man had to ask him a lot of questions and he got tongue-tied and could not give clear answers. The man did not smile at all. He went off and a minute later came and fetched André to a big office. A black-haired man with glasses was sitting at a desk. On both sides of the desk were telephones and panels of push-buttons. There was a carpet on the floor and huge leather easy chairs. The whole of one wall was a large and exciting circuit map with flickering coloured lights showing where the power was going all over the country.

André did not say five words before his lip began trembling and two tears rolled out of his eyes. The man told him, 'Sit down, son, and don't be scared.'

Then the man tried to explain. How could they cut off the power when thousands and thousands of machines were running on electricity? He pointed with the back of his pencil at the circuit map. If there were a shutdown the power would have to be rerouted, and that meant calling in other power stations and putting a heavy load on the lines. Without current for one minute the trains would stop, hospitals would go dark in the middle of an operation, the mine skips would suddenly halt twelve thousand feet down. He knew André was worried about the swallow, only things like that just happened and that was life.

'Life?' André said, thinking it was more like death.

The big man smiled. He took down the boy's name and address, and he said, 'You've done your best, André. I'm sorry I can't promise you anything.'

Downstairs again, Gas Makabeni let him out at the gate. 'Are they switching off the power?' Gas asked.

'No.'

'*Mayi babo!*' Gas shook his head and clicked. But he did not smile this time. He could see the boy was very unhappy.

André got home hours late and his mother was frantic. He lied to her too, saying he had been detained after school. He kept his eyes away from the powerline and did not have the stomach to look for the swallow. He felt so bad about it because they were all letting it die. Except for the other swallows that brought it food it would be dead already.

And that was life, the man said . . .

It must have been the middle of the night when he woke up. His mother was in the room and the light was on.

'There's a man come to see you,' she said. 'Did you ask anyone to come here?'

'No, Mama,' he said, dazed.

'Get up and come.' She sounded cross and he was scared stiff. He went out on to the stoep⁵ and there he saw his father in

---

⁵**stoep**   a covered platform running along the front of a house

his pyjamas and the back of a big man in brown overalls with ESCOM on them: a black man. It was Gas Makabeni!

'Gas!' he shouted. 'Are they going to do it?'

'They're doing it,' Gas said.

A linesman and a truck driver came up the steps on the stoep. The linesman explained to André's father a maintenance switch-down had been ordered at minimum-load hour. He wanted to be shown where the bird was. André glanced, frightened, at his father who nodded and said, 'Show him.'

He went in the maintenance truck with the man and the driver and Gas. It took them only five minutes to get the truck in position under the tower. The maintenance man checked the time and they began running up the extension ladder. Gas hooked a chain in his broad belt and pulled on his flashlight helmet. He swung out on the ladder and began running up it as if he had no weight at all. Up level with the pylon insulators, his flashlight picked out the swallow hanging on the dead wire. He leaned over and carefully worked the bird's tiny claw loose from the wire binding and then he put the swallow in the breast pocket of his overalls.

In a minute he was down again and he took the bird out and handed it to the boy. André could see even in the light of the flashlamp that the swallow had faint grey fringes round the edges of its shining blue-black feathers and that meant it was a young bird. This was its first year. He was almost speechless, holding the swallow in his hands and feeling its slight quiver.

'Thanks,' he said. 'Thanks, Gas. Thanks, sir.'

His father took the swallow from him at the house and went off to find a box to keep it out of reach of the cats.

'Off you go to bed now,' the mother said. 'You've had quite enough excitement for one day.'

The swallow drank thirstily but would not eat anything, so the parents thought it best to let it go as soon as it would fly. André took the box to his fort near the gum tree and looked towards the koppie and the powerline. It was early morning and dew sparkled on the overhead wires and made the whole level veld gleam like a magic inland sea. He held the swallow in his cupped hands and it lay there quiet with the tips of its wings crossed. Suddenly it took two little jumps with its tiny claws and spread its slender wings. Frantically they beat the air. The bird seemed to be dropping to the ground. Then it skimmed forward only a foot above the grass.

He remembered long afterwards how, when it really took wing and began to gain height, it gave a little shiver of happiness, as if it knew it was free.

Further reading

If you enjoyed considering the political issues linked to this story, look also at the story *Out of Bounds* in this collection (page 7). This deals more directly with the effect of apartheid on relationships between children in South Africa.

How to Beat the System (Texas, USA)

by Robert West

This fascinating text is from *Out of the Night: Writings from Death Row* (New Clarion Press, 1994), a collection of writing from prisoners on Death Row, edited by Marie Roberts and the poet Benjamin Zephaniah. Many countries have rejected the death penalty as part of their justice system, but in the USA around 3,500 men and 65 women currently face execution, waiting to die by electric chair, gas chamber, firing squad, lethal injection or hanging. Most of these people have committed dreadful crimes, many of them have suffered dreadful poverty and abuse in their earlier lives, and some of them are innocent. In a study conducted by Amnesty International it was discovered that over a period of 70 years, 26 men executed in the USA were later found to be innocent of all charges.

Death Row is the ultimate limitation on personal freedom. Many of these people lose touch with their families and have no visitors. Information about Robert West's difficult childhood and violent acts is shocking but in the final years of his life, unbelievable though it may sound, he discovered reading literature and writing and this brought about a remarkable change in his outlook and behaviour.

This text was written for young people all over the world; so here is some advice to you from a man who lost his freedom.

If I remember right, at 2.30 a.m. I used to be sleeping, or at least looking for a place to sleep. Sometimes stepping out into life without a sense of direction just don't go the way our strange desires would like it to, as it didn't with me.

But now, at 2.30 a.m., I don't have to worry about finding a place to sleep because here on Death Row the police take care of that. Right now it's breakfast time and the only worry I have is making it through another day.

When I was 13 years old the courts started sending me to these detention centers[1] and while I was there they told me a whole lot of stuff I didn't want to hear, didn't want to hear because I knew better. Know what I mean? just about everybody was covering up my crimes with a whole bunch of excuses, but with me it was just fun, at least that's how it started. Then I got locked up with people that needed crime to survive, and some that needed it to get attention. But none of that really matters does it? Once we're in, we're in, right? Wrong!

My day starts at 2.30 a.m. in this 5′ by 9′ cell. Across the bars they have put up some thick chicken wire so I can't throw anything on anybody. At least that's what they said it was for, to me it's just something to keep me from looking them in the eye when they come by. Makes it real hard to see the TV too.

After our small, tasteless breakfast, nothing happens till 8 a.m. Can't really listen to the radio because the police play games with the antenna. Now if ya like listening to loud church services at 3 a.m. everything's cool, Jesus stations come in real clear. Since I like acid rock[2] I'm in trouble, I'm not allowed to do what I want anymore.

On this prearranged schedule we are forced to follow, we go outside first. This means regardless of weather conditions, cold and rain included, we have three hours to play basketball or sit around and look stupid. We used to have rubber horse shoes, and a volley ball net, but they were destroyed in an attempt to get at the police. The horse shoe stakes were bent down in the ground because somebody was about to get thrown down on top of one of them. Instead, he got choked and stabbed in the middle of the yard. I watched.

Before I start detailing the perverse acts of hatred that go on in here, I want you to know that I'm not talking for the system, I'm talking against, and about, what the system does to us

---

[1]**detention centers**   prisons for young people
[2]**acid rock**   a form of rock music that was popular in the 1960s and 1970s, similar to heavy metal

without telling us why. I also want you to know that if you're going to come out of there on the right foot, you're going to have to make some decisions on your own. The system doesn't care, matter of fact they would love to have you. The choice is yours, and if you'll only slow the cool act down for a moment, you'll realize that you do have the tools it takes to beat the system. What I'm suggesting doesn't have nothing to do with waiting for 5 years to pass, because if you let your youth slip away in these centers, you'll probably end up in the cell next to me, accompanying me in my/our wait for death.

Right now you're thinking, 'What are you Mad Dog crazy?! I'll never wind up on Death Row.' Saying that reminds me of me when I was going in and out of the centers, listening to the staff put me down and falling deeper and deeper into their trap. It finally took me two trips to prison and this death sentence to realize I did what they wanted. I stopped caring about myself.

You have to understand that you have the potential to do anything you want. You are somebody, regardless of what any of those jealous people tell you. All they want to do is keep you on the bottom with them.

One of the worst things they did to me was allow me to think education was for the do-gooders. Actually, education is the ONLY road to success, so while I fought against it they laughed. I lost.

In the summer of '84, what I already thought was a bad place took a turn for the worse. There had been quite a few stabbings and bombings happening here on Death Row. We were killing each other because we let the police put bad jackets on innocent people. The police figured that as long as they could keep us fighting amongst ourselves, we would never have the time to arm ourselves with education, or do battle with the system. After a few stabbings the system let the news media start calling us animals, the public responded with their usual alarm, then the police came shaking us down for weapons. This is called creating a situation then putting an end to it so the police can say they have everything under control. They make fools out of us because we are divided and stupid. By doing that they are also getting a little more money for security purposes, but we know that's not what it's always used for.

During the shake down they tore up our personal property, including photos of our families, any crafts or hobbies we might have been passing the time with, books and legal papers. Of course some of us were mad enough to fight, and fight we did. Although I wasn't alone, I speak of my own battles that followed. Listen close because what may sound cool was nothing but a losing situation for me, as it always is when we practice violence instead of using our minds.

Upon returning to my cell, I found what little property I was allowed to have had been senselessly destroyed and the entire cell was trashed. Instead of salvaging what I could, I kicked the sink and toilet off the wall and went to throwing chunks of porcelain[3] at the police. Just when I thought I was going to get even, they approached my cell wearing flak jackets[4] and helmets, carrying shields, clubs and a shock gun. For the moment, and as is always the case, they had won because I was out-numbered and out-weaponed.

I was handcuffed behind my back and led to solitary[5] where I ended up staying for 45 days. In solitary we were allowed nothing except for writing material and a pair of boxer shorts. Nothing to smoke, warm water to drink and what they gave us to eat, which was very little.

In early October I was moved from solitary back to the cell-block. From there things settled down (football season ya know?) then went crazy again after the Superbowl.

The second major shake down happened at the end of January, and once again they tore our property to pieces. This time we resorted to the largest uprising in Texas Death Row

---

[3]**porcelain**   hard but delicate white substance used for making cups, plates, sinks and toilets
[4]**flak jacket**   a special piece of clothing worn by soldiers and police to protect them from bullets and weapons
[5]**solitary**   solitary prison confinement where prisoners are kept separately from other people

history. (Which doesn't say much for the rebels here before us.) From our cells we pulled 4 TVs off of the wall, set the barber chair on fire, broke out all of the windows, flooded all three tiers, and set enough fires to half choke everybody on the smoke. Several officers were assaulted with human waste as our cells riot lasted for 18 hours.

When it was time to move I was picked up by the shackles,[6] cuffs,[7] hair and throat, then used as a battering ram from my cell to the day room. All of this time, and until the end, my toes and fingers were bent as well as twisted.

In the day room I was slammed face first on the floor, a knee was mashed on the back of my head, in the small of my back and across my ankles. At that time nurse M— examined me, although she couldn't see much of me on the bottom of the pile. Without even touching me she gave the word that I was 'OK' and the beating could continue. From the day room I was carried by the cuffs, hair, throat, toes and fingers, to a gurney[8] that waited in the outside main hall. This was for all of the population inmates to see so they could be scared by the violence. It worked because they all stepped far to the side, allowing the beating to continue. Nobody gave a damn about the excessive use of force being displayed because 1) It wasn't happening to them. Yet. 2) The system had done taken the care and concern out of their battered emotions.

The people in this prison are nothing but shells of what they used to be. You are in part one of this inner death right now. The detention centers are where these seeds are planted, but their growth is up to you.

As I went down the hall on the gurney, the toes and fingers were still twisted. My feet were bent up to the back of my head while my hair was pulled and my throat was squeezed.

In front of the solitary wing I was lifted by the shackles, cuffs, hair, throat, fingers and toes, then used as a battering

[6]**shackles**   a pair of metal rings connected by a chain and fastened to a person's wrists or ankles to prevent them from escaping
[7]**cuffs**   informal term for handcuffs
[8]**gurney**   a light bed on wheels

ram all the way to the end of the second tier. In the cell I was slammed to the floor and piled on again, getting punched and kicked while the cuffs and shackles were beat back off. After a few more moments of beating my shorts were ripped off, and to nobody's surprise they were full of shit. They laughed, giggled and humiliated me as they ran out of the cell one at a time, leaving me full of cuts, bumps, bruises and fractured joints.

Two years later my joints still aren't the same, but that's probably because I've had my butt kicked twice since then.

On top of that physical abuse they play head games, like what you're probably experiencing now but don't really understand, as far as their long term effects are concerned. Their best game is allowing you to think you're worthless and even going so far as to make you believe it, instead of showing you that you're not.

You do have options. You can get away from this criminal bullshit and make a life for yourself through positive means, or you can keep giving the system a reason to exist by reserving a cell next to mine. There's more than enough ass-kicking and humiliating to go around.

Now if you really want to beat the system, you'll do more damage by staying out of it than you can ever do in it. It all comes down to YOU. YOU can either scream and cry about how bad you have it, which is really nothing but a sign of weakness and stupidity, or you can reach inside of yourself, grab those precious dreams and make them come true. YOU must first realize what YOU want to be, what YOU want to do. Your reach is limitless because you possess something they cannot steal. Youth, strength, and a mind that thinks for YOU.

Well, I do have things to do. I'm trying to finish a book I started so I can call myself a writer. When I'm writing in it I can't help but wonder where I might be if I would have started writing the first time I was put in a detention center. Or if I would have asked one of my teachers for directions into a career, and trusted somebody for a change instead of stealing that too.

Guess this is just what happens when ya sit back and watch life go by, instead of getting involved in it.

There is nothing but pain in here. Do you want some?

Robert West was executed on 27 July 1997.

Further reading

If you would like to read some of the poetry written by prisoners on Death Row, have a look at the book from which *How to Beat the System* is taken: *Out of the Night: Writings from Death Row*, edited by Marie Roberts and Benjamin Zephaniah (New Clarion Press, 1994).

Activities

Zlata's Diary

Before you read

1   The first text is an introduction to *Zlata's Diary* by the reporter Krishnan Guru-Murthy. Discuss with the rest of your class the purpose of an introduction to a book.
   ● What is it for?
   ● What information would you expect to find there?
   ● What effect should it have on the reader?

What's it about?

Read Krishnan Guru-Murthy's introduction and answer questions 2 and 3 by yourself. Then compare your answers with a partner's.

2   **a** What is the purpose of paragraph one?
   b How does the author appeal to the reader's senses in this paragraph and why does he do it?

3   What facts does the author use to establish Zlata as a normal young person? Copy out some relevant quotations and explain your choices.

Thinking about the text

Now read the extracts from *Zlata's Diary* and answer questions 4 and 5.

4   Working with a partner, select evidence from *Zlata's Diary* that reflects what Guru-Murthy tells us about her in the introduction. Use a table like the one below. An example is done for you:

Krishnan Guru-Murthy	Zlata
The journalist mentions that friends are an important part of Zlata's life.	She mentions looking forward to seeing her friends at the beginning of her diary, but there is no mention of them at the end when she is experiencing the effects of the war. As she begins a new term she says, 'I'm glad we'll be together again'.

5   Guru-Murthy refers to Zlata's diary as her 'passport to freedom'.
   ● What does this mean?
   ● What technique is the writer using here?

Cruelty to Children

Before you read

1   Some people believe that childhood is the happiest time in a person's life. Working with a partner, write a list of words and phrases that describe an ideal picture of a perfect childhood.

2   Think of one of your happiest memories of childhood. Describe it to the rest of your class.

What's it about?

Read the text and write down your answers to questions 3 to 5.

3   Write a paragraph summarising Narayan's criticisms of the school system. Use quotations to support your answer.

4   What does Narayan believe childhood should be like? Find a quotation to support your answer.

5   In the first paragraph of his speech, Narayan uses the verbs 'pulled', 'got ready', 'groomed' and 'stuffed'. What kind of verbs are they and how do they convey Narayan's point of view?

Thinking about the text

6   The following techniques are often found in powerful speeches. Working with a partner, copy the list and tick the techniques which are used by Narayan. Find a quotation to illustrate each one.

- emotive language
- humorous language and imagery
- exaggeration
- use of the imperative
- talking positively about the future
- logical argument
- political or legal language
- repetition
- supporting evidence such as statistics or real-life stories

Write your own powerful and humorous speech about the plight of teenagers in society, entitled 'Cruelty to teenagers'. Use some of the techniques listed in question 6 above and anything you have learned from reading Narayan's speech. You might want to focus on one aspect of teenage life in particular (e.g. the school dinner system, dating, leisure activities). Practise your speech, then deliver it to the rest of your class.

Guess Who Is Coming to Dinner

Before you read

1   Think about your personal identity. When you meet someone for the first time they will make assumptions about you. As you reveal information about yourself, their impression will change. Discuss the questions below with a partner.

   ● What three things about your own identity are you most keen to share with other people your own age when you first meet them?
   ● What do adults usually think of you, on first impression? Is this correct?

What's it about?

Read the story and answer questions 2 to 4 by yourself. Then discuss your ideas in a small group.

2   The first two paragraphs reveal information about the narrator's viewpoint.

   ● Summarise in a sentence what the narrator thinks about English middle-class housewives.
   ● What word would you use to describe the tone of the opening of the story? Give reasons for your answer.

3   How is the housewife rude to the narrator during the conversation about language and travel on pages 134–135?

4   'The waves of humiliation swept through me like a thunderstorm'. What device does the narrator use here and what does it show about how she feels about the dinner party?

Thinking about the text

5   '"Yes, I am a lawyer," I simply said.' Why is this line important to the story and how does it make you feel? Discuss your response with a partner, then share your ideas with the rest of your class.

6   Imagine that the hostess's husband also attended this dinner party. Working with a partner, write down what the hostess did wrong and what she could do to make her guest more comfortable. Then, improvise a conversation between the hosts, in which the husband points out what his wife did wrong and how she could change. Using your knowledge of the hostess, think about how she might react to her husband's comments.

The Mailed Parcel

Before you read

1 What does the word 'parcel' make you feel? What do you associate it with? How often do you receive something in the post, and do you enjoy this experience? How might this change once you are an adult?

What's it about?

Read the story and answer questions 2 to 5 by yourself. Then compare your answers with a partner's.

2 Read paragraph one again. What does it tell you about the characters and setting? What questions does it raise in the reader's mind?

3 In paragraph two, we follow the man's thought processes about the parcel. Summarise in your own words the reasons why he is suspicious of the parcel.

4 Think carefully about the perspective this story is written from.
   ● Is the story written in the first person, the second person or the third person?
   ● What are the names of the central characters in the story?
   ● Why do you think the author has made these choices?

5 Read the paragraph beginning 'Here they had found security' (page 139) again. Identify the words and phrases that convey the couple's past and comment on what they suggest about their feelings.

Thinking about the text

6 Working in a small group, think about the last line of the story. Why do you think the characters react as they do? Why is this parcel likened to a bomb?

7 Working in a small group, think about the hardships that this refugee family have endured. Make a list of the hardships they have faced in the past and those they are still facing.

Power

Before you read

1   In a small group discuss the meaning of the word 'compassion' and a time when *each of you* thinks you have acted with compassion.

2   Look at the picture of a pylon on page 144. What does this image immediately suggest to you? Jot down some words and share them with a partner.

What's it about?

Read the story and answer questions 3 to 5 by yourself. Then discuss your ideas in a small group.

3   The beginning of this story describes André's home background. Which of the following words do you think best describe André's life?

trapped	*lonely*	*unhappy*	*misunderstood*
peaceful	*angry*	*curious*	

4   Scan the first two pages of this story. What does André find attractive about the pylons?

5   Re-read André's thoughts about the swallows on page 146: 'They were going . . . dreamt of.' What differences does the writer see between the power of the pylons and the power of the swallows?

Thinking about the text

6   What reasons might André's parents have for being so reluctant to do anything about the trapped swallow? Look through the text and identify where they discourage André from thinking about it. In pairs, prepare a two-minute conversation between the parents that reflects their thoughts and feelings about the situation. Use these questions to help you:
   ● Do André's parents not love him?
   ● Are they hard and uncaring people?
   ● Are they unwilling to deal with big and more important issues outside their own lives?

   Perform your drama to the class.

7   Read the last two paragraphs of the story again. Is this a satisfactory ending to the story? Write a paragraph explaining your answer.

How to Beat the System

Before you read

1   In many American states, the punishment for the most serious crimes is the death penalty. What do you know about this issue? Whether or not you know much about it, what is your personal viewpoint? Discuss your ideas with the rest of your class.

2   In a small group, discuss the word 'justice'. What does it mean? Which people represent justice in the society you live in?

What's it about?

Read the text and answer questions 3 to 5 by yourself. Then compare your answers with a partner's.

3   Paragraph three focuses on the writer's first experiences of crime and detention centres. What does he tell you about his personality and motivations when he was young?

4   What kinds of abuse did West experience during his time in prison around summer 1984?

5   Read the paragraph that begins 'Now if you really want to beat the system' (page 161) again. Summarise Robert West's advice to young people in your own words.

Thinking about the text

6   How effective an ending is the final sentence of this piece? Write a paragraph explaining your answer.

7   West presents his advice in an informal style, as though he is talking to his reader. Write down some examples of this kind of language and explain why he uses this style.

8   Research the issues surrounding the death penalty and write your own persuasive speech arguing for or against this issue. You might like to start by visiting this website:
http://www.deathpenaltyinfo.org/

Compare and contrast

1   This section looks at many aspects of personal freedom, including isolation, being a refugee and apartheid. Choose one such aspect and create a collage to illustrate your theme. Use images and quotations from the texts as well as relevant newspaper cuttings and snippets of your own personal response. Write a paragraph explaining your choices.

2   The wide geographical spread of the texts from this section reflects the importance of personal freedom to human existence. Working in a small group, pick one of the issues raised in the texts (e.g. the death penalty, children's rights, apartheid) and research it. Then prepare a presentation that explains the social and historical context of two of the texts to the class. In your presentation, comment on how your findings have helped your understanding of the two texts of your choice.

3   The three texts *Cruelty to Children, How to Beat the System* and *Guess Who Is Coming to Dinner* are written with a strong authorial voice. Working in a small group, identify the audience and purpose of each piece of writing. Discuss how the language and style of each first-person narrative is appropriate to its audience and purpose. Make sure you identify words and phrases that support your argument.

4   Which of the texts in this section has affected you most through its portrayal of a political or moral point? What techniques did the writer use to affect you? Make some notes by yourself, then discuss your ideas in a small group. See if you can agree a 'top two' to share with the rest of your class.

5   Choose your favourite and least favourite text. Find out a little bit about the authors and then write a short letter to each of them. Tell the author a bit about yourself and give your personal response to their text, then ask any questions you might have about the text.

4 Cultural traditions

The texts in the first three sections of this collection originate in a wide range of countries. They offer us an insight into different settings and experiences but, despite the differences they highlight, many also emphasise human connections, shared needs and what we all, as humans, have in common. This section focuses on aspects of certain cultures that are distinct and different. The prose and poetry here cover a range of topics, from arts and leisure to superstitions and religion in a variety of countries.

Activities

1 'Ritual' is a word used to describe ceremonial acts or established routines. Looking back at their childhood, most people can remember formal and informal rituals – some that were part of everyday life, others connected to religious or seasonal times of celebration. What rituals are part of your home life? Discuss a couple of these with a partner.

2 What is the cultural identity of the country you live in, or the country of your own ethnic background? List the elements that make up that identity. Think about:
   - leisure pursuits
   - religious rituals
   - seasonal celebrations and holidays
   - food
   - music
   - key cultural places to visit for tourists.

Was it easy to identify the distinct traits of your own country? Why / why not? Share your list and discuss your ideas in a small group.

3   Find out about one of the following traditions. Then spend 10 minutes mingling with and speaking to other members of your class, to ensure you have found out about them all.

- What is the Jewish *kippah*?
- How is *Salaat*, the Islamic ritual prayer, performed?
- What is a Japanese tea ceremony?
- How do the Chinese celebrate New Year?
- What is the *puja* ceremony for Hindus?
- What are name days in the Czech Republic?

Film Boy (India)

by Alexander McCall Smith

This story is set in a country that has not been part of the author's own life. He uses his knowledge of the culture of India to create a realistic fiction and explore the relationship between a boy and his hero. The backdrop of the story is the film industry of Mumbai (Bombay), India. Hollywood is an important part of the identity of the USA; Bollywood (Hindi cinema) is perhaps an even more culturally important industry in India.

Fourteen million Indians go to the movies on a daily basis (about 1.4 per cent of the population of 1 billion) and pay the equivalent of the average Indian's daily wage to see one of the 800 or so films produced by Bollywood each year. Since 1971, India has been the country with the highest output of feature films.

Prem lived in Bombay. He had always lived there and he knew that Bombay was the most important city in all India. There was always so much going on – there were vast factories with smoking chimneys, shops and bazaars that seemed to go on and on for ever, and, most important of all, there were the film studios. Prem loved to go to the cinema. Sitting in his seat at the Regal Picture House, he would watch the exciting films that were made right there in Bombay.

The way Prem got the money for his cinema tickets was to work for it. Every day, after school, he would call in at the sweet stall which stood outside the nearby hospital. Mr Rahna, who owned the stall, did not have an assistant, and this made it hard for him to get away to have coffee with his friends. For half an hour or so each afternoon Prem would look after the stall for him, selling the sweetmeats[1] to passers-by and putting the money in the cash box.

'Who do you think is the best film star?' a friend asked Prem one day.

---

[1] **sweetmeats**   small pieces of food covered in sugar

Prem thought for a moment. 'Well,' he replied, 'Jani Sudha is very good. And I like Goel Prakash. But the very best, I think, is Rasi Paliwalar.'

Prem's friend looked thoughtful. 'I think you're right,' he said. 'I've heard people say he's the best in the world.'

'He is,' Prem said firmly. 'I'm sure he is.'

They had both seen many films starring Rasi and had enjoyed them all. Rasi was always the hero. If there was somebody who needed to be rescued, then Rasi would be the one to do it. It did not matter if the danger came from a flood or from a tiger, Rasi would not hesitate. Then, if the police were having difficulty in arresting a bandit, Rasi would be the person to whom they would turn. There was no limit to what he could do.

There was no mistaking Rasi. He was a tall man, with broad shoulders, and teeth that glinted like pinpoints of light when he smiled. His famous voice was deep – almost a growl when he was angry – but in the middle of a fight it could sound more like a shriek. That was a sound that would always send a shiver of fear down the spines of his enemies. Prem had often wondered what Rasi would look like in the flesh. Would he look so daring as he did on the screen? Would he look quite so impressive? Prem had no idea – that is, until the day he saw him.

This is how it happened. Prem had gone to Mr Rahna's stall at his usual time. Business was a bit quiet that day, Mr Rahna had said, and it would not have surprised Prem if he sold no sweetmeats at all. In fact, Prem might well have dozed off in the heat, had a large car not suddenly stopped in the street outside the stall and an unmistakeable figure stepped out. It was Rasi Paliwalar.

'Which of these sweets do you recommend?' the famous voice had asked.

'They're all very fresh, sir,' Prem said. His voice sounded shaky and he hoped that Rasi would not laugh.

'I'm sure they are,' Rasi replied pleasantly. 'But which taste best?'

Prem pointed out a tray of mango-flavoured[2] fudge.

---

[2]**mango**   an oval tropical fruit with a smooth skin, juicy orange-yellow flesh and a large hard seed in the middle

'Many people like that one, Mr Paliwalar.'

Rasi looked up. 'You go to the films?' he asked.

'Oh yes, sir,' Prem said. 'I go every week.'

Rasi nodded. 'Good,' he said simply. 'Now I'll take ten pieces of that mango fudge.'

Prem took the coins which Rasi offered him and handed over the sweets. Rasi smiled again and then, without saying goodbye, dashed back across the road to the waiting car. The driver pulled out into the road, changed gear, and sped off.

Prem looked at the coins in his hand. Rasi had given him three times more than he needed to pay. Many people would have kept the extra money, but not Prem. It did not matter if Mr Paliwalar was rich – which he undoubtedly was. The extra money belonged to the film star, and Prem was determined that he would get it back. Besides, if he gave it back to him, Prem would have the chance to meet his hero again, and that was something he would like very much indeed.

Bombay is a great city. There are millions of people living there and to find one person out of all those millions is not simple. Eventually, though, Prem found out where Rasi lived and made his way to the wealthy street of great houses. His heart sank as he saw the gates of Rasi's mansion. They were twice as tall as he was and topped with menacing iron spikes. The garden wall, which ran along the edge of the road, was just as high and was also spiked. It was clear that the only way into the house was by invitation.

Prem walked up to the gates and peered shyly through the bars. Just inside the garden there was a small shed, from which an attendant immediately appeared.

'Go away,' he shouted, gesturing angrily. 'Get away from here.'

Prem drew back. 'I want to see Mr Paliwalar,' he shouted out, trying not to seem too frightened of the guard's unwelcoming manner.

'You want to see Mr Paliwalar,' the guard sneered. 'The whole world wants to see Mr Paliwalar. You can go and see him in the cinema any day. Now run along!'

'But I've got to give him something,' Prem persisted. 'I must see him.'

The guard shook his head. 'Don't waste my time, little boy. Now are you going to go away or am I going to have to come out and beat you with my stick?'

Prem looked nervously at the stout pole that the guard was carrying. As keen as he was to see Rasi, he was not going to argue with that particular guard. No, there must be a less risky way of getting through.

'All right,' he said. 'Don't worry. I'm going away.'

He did not go away, though. Just at that moment, a delivery truck arrived and sounded its horn. As the guard opened the gates to let the truck enter, Prem shot in on the other side. Nobody saw him do it, and nobody saw him creep up to the great house and on to its shady verandah. There was a large glass door that led off the verandah and into the house. As Prem peered in, he heard distant notes of music coming from deep within. There was certainly somebody at home – probably the film star himself.

Prem decided to knock on the glass door. It was not a loud knock and it was completely lost in the vast entrance hall that lay beyond. He knocked again, more firmly this time, but the sound still seemed too faint. Gently, he pushed open the door and stepped inside.

Prem looked about the entrance hall. It was a magnificently furnished room, hung with brightly coloured weavings and ivory trophies. A tiger's head with fixed, glaring eyes was mounted on one wall, and on another there was the stuffed head of an antelope.

Quietly he moved through the hall and into the room beyond. This was a living room, a room which stretched out in all directions. At one end there was a large piano topped with vases of flowers, at another end there were sofas and chairs covered with zebra skin. In the middle of the room there was a marble mosaic floor in the shape of a giant star, with each point a different colour.

Prem stood in silent wonderment. He had seen rooms like this in films, but he had never imagined that there would be such places right here in Bombay. He pictured the parties which must have taken place in this room – the swirl of colour from the pure silk saris, the laughter, the tinkling of ice in glasses, the music . . .

'Thief!' a voice rasped behind him. 'It's no good running. I've locked the door!'

The servant had entered the room so quietly that Prem had been quite unaware of his presence. The first thing he had felt was the tight grip on his arms and the sudden pain as they were forced behind his back. Then he heard the voice of his captor and the awful accusation.

Prem struggled to free himself, but this only made the servant push his arms higher. There was no point in resisting, he thought; I'm trapped.

'I'm not a thief,' he shouted out. 'I'm here to see Mr Paliwalar.'

'Don't lie to me!' the servant hissed. 'I know you thieving boys. We've caught you before.'

'I'm not lying,' Prem persisted. 'I knocked on the door. There was no reply.'

'Ah!' cried the servant, twisting Prem's arm. 'A thief who knocks on the door! A very polite thief!'

The pressure on Prem's arms suddenly slackened, although he was still tightly held. Prem felt himself being turned round and then frog-marched out of the room.

'Where are you taking me?' he asked. 'You must let me go.'

The servant laughed. 'Oh we'll let you go. Certainly we'll let you go. Once the police have arrived, we'll let you go then.'

They crossed the hall and went through a small door that led towards the back of the house.

'Please don't twist my arm,' Prem begged the servant. 'I won't run away now.'

The servant relaxed the pressure slightly and Prem made no move to escape. Sensing this, the servant's grip became even slacker. It was at this moment that Prem saw his chance. They had reached a point in the corridor where a staircase wound off on one side. It was the only possible escape that had presented itself so far and Prem took it. Wresting³ his arms free, he hurled himself away from the servant, pushing him over as he did so. There was a shout and a crash as the servant stumbled and Prem leapt up the stairs.

'Thief!' shouted the enraged voice below him. 'Thief!'

Prem mounted the stairs three at a time. Reaching the top, he saw that he was in another corridor. There were no windows, he noticed, and so he decided to run headlong wherever the corridor took him. There were two doors at the end, one of them ajar, the other closed. Prem pushed open the door which was slightly ajar and then slammed it shut behind him. Turning round, he bent over to recover his breath. When he looked up, he saw that there was a man sitting writing at a desk near the window.

³**wresting**   violently pulling something away from someone

Rasi Paliwalar spun round in astonishment. From down the corridor there came the sound of running feet and the voice of the angry servant.

'Mr Paliwalar! Mr Paliwalar! There's a thief loose in the house!'

Rasi laid down his pen and stared hard at Prem.

'So,' he said coldly. 'So we have a thief.'

Prem stood where he was, unable to move, unable to speak. Behind him the door opened sharply and the servant burst in breathlessly.

'Here he is, Mr Paliwalar. I have caught him now.'

Prem felt the man's grip again and winced in pain. His arms were forced up behind his back, almost lifting him off his feet.

'No!' he shouted. 'I'm not a thief! I'm not!'

As Prem screamed out, Rasi rose from his desk.

'Let him go,' he said to the servant. 'You don't have to half kill him.'

The servant released his grip reluctantly and Prem felt the blood surge back into his arms. Rasi was looking at him curiously and he realised that this was his opportunity to explain.

'I'm not a thief, Mr Paliwalar,' Prem blurted out. 'I came to see you. You remember me.'

Rasi raised an eyebrow. 'Remember you? I don't know you, do I?'

Prem lowered his eyes. 'You came to our sweetmeat stall a few days ago. Near the hospital. I served you.'

Rasi was silent. 'Maybe,' he said. 'Maybe I did.'

'He's lying, sir,' the servant interrupted. 'These boys lie and lie again. You mustn't believe him.'

'Quiet!' Rasi snapped. 'Let him have his say.'

Slowly, and stumbling over parts of the story, Prem told Rasi why he had wanted to see him. As he spoke, he thought how far-fetched the story sounded – if he had been in Rasi's place, would he believe that somebody would go to all that trouble just to return a few coins?

Suddenly the servant interrupted.

'If this is true, Mr Paliwalar,' he said. 'Then let him show us this money. That will prove it.'

Rasi looked at Prem inquisitively. 'Well?' he said. 'Why don't you show us this famous money?'

Prem smiled. 'Of course.' Then, dipping into his trouser pocket he felt for the familiar coins. For a moment his heart stopped. There was nothing there.

'Well?' urged Rasi. 'Let's see the money.'

Prem struggled to utter his reply. It was the end of his world now; nobody would believe him – he would be labelled a thief.

'I've lost it, Mr Paliwalar. I had it in my pocket, but it must have fallen out in the garden. I promise you it was there. I promise you . . . ' He tailed off, his voice becoming weaker.

'Ha!' shouted the servant. 'You see, Mr Paliwalar! I was right!'

Rasi looked at Prem and shook his head.

'It doesn't look good for you, does it?' he said quietly.

'No,' said Prem. 'But I promise you, Mr Paliwalar, I'm not a thief.'

Rasi was quiet for a moment. Then he looked at the servant and issued an instruction.

'Take this young man outside,' he said. 'Let him show you where he was in the garden. If he doesn't find the money, then you can call the police. If he finds it, then call me. Do you understand?'

The servant nodded. Holding firmly on to Prem's wrist, he led him out of the room and down the corridor.

The servant standing over him, Prem searched through the garden for the missing money. There was no sign of it, and soon the servant dragged him back into the house. There is one last chance, thought Prem: the stairs. The money might well have fallen there when he had made his dash up the stairs.

The servant tried to prevent him, but Prem managed to drag himself to the foot of the staircase. This was where he had launched himself away and this is where he had gone down on his hands and knees. It was exactly the sort of place where something might have fallen out of his pocket.

And that is just what had happened. There, on the third stair from the bottom, the coins lay where they had fallen, three small circles of metal, but in Prem's eyes the most welcome sight imaginable.

'I've found them!' Prem shouted. 'See! I told you that I had them!'

The servant looked at the coins suspiciously. 'Maybe they were dropped by somebody else,' he said. 'People are always coming and going on these stairs.'

'They're mine!' Prem protested. 'It's exactly the amount I told Mr Paliwalar I had. There, count them!'

He handed the coins to the servant, who looked at them doubtfully.

'No,' said the servant. 'These are not your coins. I myself lost some money on these stairs. These coins are mine.'

And with that, he slipped the coins into his pocket and reached out to grab Prem's arm.

'You're coming with me to the kitchen,' he said. 'We'll wait there for the police.'

'Let me go!' Prem shouted. 'I've found the money. Mr Paliwalar said you were to take me to him! Let me go!'

Prem fought against the servant's grasp but he was unable to free himself. He kicked at the man's shins, but missed, and was only rewarded with a hard blow to his chest. It's no use, he said to himself – there's nothing I can do.

And then he saw Mr Paliwalar standing above him on the stairs.

'Mr Paliwalar,' he shouted, 'I . . . '

Rasi raised a hand to silence him.

'I heard all that,' he said, his eyes fixed on the servant. 'You can let this young man go. I'll speak to you later.'

The servant dropped Prem's arm and shuffled off down the corridor. Prem looked back up at Rasi and noticed that he was smiling.

'I'm sorry I didn't believe you,' Rasi said, as he came down the stairs to where Prem was standing. 'I hope you'll let me make it up to you. I think that I owe you rather more than an apology. Don't you?'

Prem said nothing. Then Mr Paliwalar went on:

'How about a visit to the studio?' he said. 'You'd like that, wouldn't you? What about next week?'

The following Friday, Rasi's car arrived at the promised time and Prem climbed in beside the driver. Half an hour later they were at the studio gate, a large, impressive set of pillars with the name of the film company written in gold letters over the top. The guard at the gate waved Rasi's car through and the driver nosed slowly into a parking place near a large building.

'Mr Paliwalar will meet you in his dressing room,' he said. 'If you go over to that booth they'll show you where to go.'

The dressing room had Rasi's name written on it. Prem bent down to dust his shoes and then, as confidently as he could, he knocked on the door. After a moment, the door was flung open by an assistant, who looked at Prem with irritation. He was about to tell Prem to go away when, from within the room, there came a shout.

'If that's my friend Prem,' Rasi called out, 'then show him in.'

As Prem entered the room, Rasi rose to his feet. He looked splendid. On his head he had a brilliant red turban, with flowing sash, and at his side he wore a wicked-looking curved sword.

'I'm playing a lancer today,' he explained, gesturing at the uniform. 'Come. Let's see what my director wants me to do.'

Prem and Rasi made their way through the echoing studios. All about, there were signs of feverish activity. Lights hung suspended from beams, camera tracks criss-crossed the floor and people rushed about with props and costumes. In one corner of the studio, a set had been made up to look like the deck of a boat, and two actors were busy heaving on ropes under the glare of the lights. In another part, a large black car was being edged into position in front of a garage set and several actors dressed as policemen were standing by, ready for filming.

'We're filming outside,' Rasi explained, as they left the main studio building. 'I think I'm meant to be rescuing somebody from a fortress. It'll be hot work!'

When they reached the mock-up of the fortress, Prem stood to one side as Rasi discussed his role with the director and his assistants. Then, when the other actors were in place, a man with a striped clapperboard[4] stood in front of the cameras and brought the clapper down with a sharp snap. Rasi, who had mounted a horse, now rode up to the fortress in a cloud of dust. The most exciting two hours of Prem's life had just begun.

Several months later, Rasi's new film was released. Prem saw the posters advertising it go up outside the Regal Picture House and his heart swelled with pride at the thought that he had seen the filming.

The day before the film was due to be shown for the first time, Prem went to work as usual at the sweetmeat stand. Mr Rahna, who was expecting him, gave him a broad smile.

'Well, well,' he said genially. 'So there you are!'

'I hope I'm not late,' Prem said, glancing at the watch on Mr Rahna's wrist.

'Oh, you're not late,' Mr Rahna reassured him. 'It's just that somebody called to see you. A friend of yours.'

Prem was puzzled. He could not imagine who might come to see him at the stall, or at least who would bother Mr Rahna on his account.

'Yes,' went on Mr Rahna. 'A very well known friend . . . '

Prem caught his breath. Could it be? Dared he hope?

'Here,' said Mr Rahna. 'He left this for you.'

Prem took the envelope from Mr Rahna's hand and examined it carefully.

---

[4]**clapperboard**   a device used by people making films consisting of a board with two parts which are hit together at the start of filming

'Go on,' urged Mr Rahna. 'Open it!'

Prem eased open the envelope flap. Inside was a letter with another piece of paper attached to it. He glanced quickly at the bottom of the page to see the signature:

Rasi Paliwalar.

'You see!' crowed Mr Rahna. 'Mr Paliwalar himself came round with that! With my own eyes I saw him! I shook his hand!' He paused. 'And what does he say? Come on!'

Prem read the letter and smiled.

'It's two free tickets for the first Bombay showing of his new film,' he said. 'He also says he might see me again one day if he's passing this way.'

'Oh my!' exclaimed Mr Rahna. 'Two free tickets to the premiere! Who'll go with you?'

Prem paused and thought for a moment. There was really no doubt in his mind as to whom he should invite.

'You,' he said simply, and then: 'That is, if you'd like to go.'

'Would I like to go!' shouted Mr Rahna. 'Of course I'd like to go!'

As he spoke, Mr Rahna emerged from behind the counter and shook Prem by the hand.

'Oh my goodness!' he said, his voice becoming high with excitement. 'What an exciting occasion that will be!'

'Yes,' said Prem. 'It will.'

And that is just what it turned out to be. As Prem sat in the darkness of the cinema, Mr Rahna at his side, he watched with pride as the great rescue scene came up on the screen. 'One day,' he muttered to himself, 'I'm going to work in that film studio.'

'Did you say something?' Mr Rahna asked.

Prem shook his head. Some plans, like some secrets, are best kept to ourselves.

Further reading

A popular children's author who sets many of her novels in India is Jamila Gavin. Try *Grandpa Chatterji's Third Eye* (Egmont Books, 2006) or *Wheel of Surya* (Egmont Books, 2001).

First Confession (Ireland)

by Frank O'Connor

This story is set in Frank O'Connor's homeland of Ireland. He describes the rites and practices of the Catholic religion from the point of view of a young boy. Confession is the Catholic practice of telling a priest the things you have done wrong, before taking communion. The story focuses on the young boy's experience of his first confession and how his confused beliefs about this practice are formed by the adults and family around him.

All the trouble began when my grandfather died and my grand-mother – my father's mother – came to live with us. Relations in the one house are a strain at the best of times, but, to make matters worse, my grandmother was a real old country woman and quite unsuited to the life in town. She had a fat, wrinkled old face, and, to Mother's great indignation,[1] went round the house in bare feet – the boots had her crippled, she said. For dinner she had a jug of porter and a pot of potatoes with – sometimes – a bit of salt fish, and she poured out the potatoes on the table and ate them slowly, with great relish, using her fingers by way of a fork.

Now, girls are supposed to be fastidious,[2] but I was the one who suffered most from this. Nora, my sister, just sucked up to the old woman for the penny she got every Friday out of the old-age pension, a thing I could not do. I was too honest, that was my trouble; and when I was playing with Bill Connell, the sergeant-major's son, and saw my grandmother steering up the path with the jug of porter sticking out from beneath her shawl I was mortified.[3] I made excuses not to let him come into the house, because I could never be sure what she would be up to when we went in.

When Mother was at work and my grandmother made the dinner I wouldn't touch it. Nora once tried to make me, but I hid

---

[1]**indignation**   being offended or angry because of something unfair or wrong
[2]**fastidious**   fussy
[3]**mortified**   very embarrassed

under the table from her and took the bread-knife with me for protection. Nora let on to be very indignant (she wasn't, of course, but she knew Mother saw through her, so she sided with Gran) and came after me. I lashed out at her with the bread-knife, and after that she left me alone. I stayed there till Mother came in from work and made my dinner, but when Father came in later Nora said in a shocked voice: 'Oh, Dadda, do you know what Jackie did at dinnertime?' Then, of course, it all came out; Father gave me a flaking; Mother interfered, and for days after that he didn't speak to me and Mother barely spoke to Nora. And all because of that old woman! God knows, I was heart-scalded.

Then, to crown my misfortunes, I had to make my first confession and Communion. It was an old woman called Ryan who prepared us for these. She was about the one age with Gran; she was well-to-do, lived in a big house on Montenotte, wore a black cloak and bonnet, and came every day to school at three o'clock when we should have been going home, and talked to us of Hell. She may have mentioned the other place as well, but that could only have been by accident, for Hell had the first place in her heart.

She lit a candle, took out a new half-crown,[4] and offered it to the first boy who would hold one finger – only one fin-ger! – in the flame for five minutes by the school clock. Being always very ambitious I was tempted to volunteer, but I thought it might look greedy. Then she asked were we afraid of holding one finger – only one finger! – in a little candle flame for five minutes and not afraid of burning all over in roasting hot fur-naces for all eternity. 'All eternity! Just think of that! A whole lifetime goes by and it's nothing, not even a drop in the ocean of your sufferings.' The woman was really interesting about Hell, but my attention was all fixed on the half-crown. At the end of the lesson she put it back in her purse. It was a great dis-appointment; a religious woman like that, you wouldn't think she'd bother about a thing like a half-crown.

---

[4]**half-crown**   old British coin worth twenty-five pence

Another day she said she knew a priest who woke one night to find a fellow he didn't recognize leaning over the end of his bed. The priest was a bit frightened – naturally enough – but he asked the fellow what he wanted, and the fellow said in a deep, husky voice that he wanted to go to Confession. The priest said it was an awkward time and wouldn't it do in the morning, but the fellow said that last time he went to Confession, there was one sin he kept back, being ashamed to mention it, and now it was always on his mind. Then the priest knew it was a bad case, because the fellow was after making a bad confession and committing a mortal sin.[5] He got up to dress, and just then the cock crew in the yard outside, and – lo and behold! – when the priest looked round there was no sign of the fellow, only a smell of burning timber, and when the priest looked at his bed didn't he see the print of two hands burned in it? That was because the fellow had made a bad confession. This story made a shocking impression on me.

But the worst of all was when she showed us how to examine our conscience. Did we take the name of the Lord, our God, in vain? Did we honor our father and our mother? (I asked her did this include grandmothers and she said it did.) Did we love our neighbor as ourselves? Did we covet our neighbor's goods? (I thought of the way I felt about the penny that Nora got every Friday.) I decided that, between one thing and another, I must have broken the whole ten commandments, all on account of that old woman, and so far as I could see, so long as she remained in the house I had no hope of ever doing anything else.

I was scared to death of Confession. The day the whole class went I let on to have a toothache, hoping my absence wouldn't be noticed; but at three o'clock, just as I was feeling safe, along comes a chap with a message from Mrs Ryan that I was to go to Confession myself on Saturday and be at the chapel for Communion with the rest. To make it worse, Mother couldn't come with me and sent Nora instead.

---

[5]**mortal sin**   in Roman Catholicism, a mortal sin is a sin that, unless confessed and absolved, condemns a person's soul to Hell after death

Now, that girl had ways of tormenting me that Mother never knew of. She held my hand as we went down the hill, smiling sadly and saying how sorry she was for me, as if she were bringing me to the hospital for an operation.

'Oh, God help us!' she moaned. 'Isn't it a terrible pity you weren't a good boy? Oh, Jackie, my heart bleeds for you! How will you ever think of all your sins? Don't forget you have to tell him about the time you kicked Gran on the shin.'

'Lemme go!' I said, trying to drag myself free of her. 'I don't want to go to Confession at all.'

'But sure, you'll have to go to Confession, Jackie,' she replied in the same regretful tone. 'Sure, if you didn't, the parish priest would be up to the house, looking for you. 'Tisn't, God knows, that I'm not sorry for you. Do you remember the time you tried to kill me with the bread-knife under the table? And the language you used to me? I don't know what he'll do with you at all, Jackie. He might have to send you up to the Bishop.'

I remember thinking bitterly that she didn't know the half of what I had to tell – if I told it. I knew I couldn't tell it, and understood perfectly why the fellow in Mrs Ryan's story made a bad confession; it seemed to me a great shame that people wouldn't stop criticizing him. I remember that steep hill down to the church, and the sunlit hillsides beyond the valley of the river, which I saw in the gaps between the houses like Adam's last glimpse of Paradise.

Then, when she had manoeuvred me down the long flight of steps to the chapel yard, Nora suddenly changed her tone. She became the raging malicious[6] devil she really was.

'There you are!' she said with a yelp of triumph, hurling me through the church door. 'And I hope he'll give you the penitential psalms,[7] you dirty little caffler.'[8]

---

[6]**malicious**   spiteful

[7]**penitential psalms**   the Penitential Psalms or Psalms of Confession is a name given to the sections of the Bible (from Psalms 6, 32, 38, 51, 102, 130 and 143) which focus on sorrow for sin

[8]**caffler**   Irish slang for an impish, rude young fellow

I knew then I was lost, given up to eternal justice. The door with the colored-glass panels swung shut behind me, the sunlight went out and gave place to deep shadow, and the wind whistled outside so that the silence within seemed to crackle like ice under my feet. Nora sat in front of me by the confession box. There were a couple of old women ahead of her, and then a miserable-looking poor devil came and wedged me in at the other side, so that I couldn't escape even if I had the courage. He joined his hands and rolled his eyes in the direction of the roof, muttering aspirations in an anguished tone, and I wondered had he a grandmother too. Only a grandmother could account for a fellow behaving in that heartbroken way, but he was better off than I, for he at least could go and confess his sins; while I would make a bad confession and then die in the night and be continually coming back and burning people's furniture.

Nora's turn came, and I heard the sound of something slamming, and then her voice as if butter wouldn't melt in her mouth, and then another slam, and out she came. God, the hypocrisy of women! Her eyes were lowered, her head was bowed, and her hands were joined very low down on her stomach, and she walked up the aisle to the side altar looking like a saint. You never saw such an exhibition of devotion and I remembered the devilish malice with which she had tormented me all the way from our door, and wondered were all religious people like that, really. It was my turn now. With the fear of damnation in my soul I went in, and the confessional door closed of itself behind me.

It was pitch-dark and I couldn't see priest or anything else. Then I really began to be frightened. In the darkness it was a matter between God and me, and He had all the odds. He knew what my intentions were before I even started; I had no chance. All I had ever been told about Confession got mixed up in my mind, and I knelt to one wall and said: 'Bless me, father, for I have sinned; this is my first confession.' I waited for a few minutes, but nothing happened, so I tried it on the other wall. Nothing happened there either. He had me spotted all right.

It must have been then that I noticed the shelf at about one height with my head. It was really a place for grown-up people to rest their elbows, but in my distracted state I thought it was probably the place you were supposed to kneel. Of course, it was on the high side and not very deep, but I was always good at climbing and managed to get up all right. Staying up was the trouble. There was room only for my knees, and nothing you could get a grip on but a sort of wooden molding[9] a bit above it. I held on to the molding and repeated the words a little louder, and this time something happened all right. A slide was slammed back; a little light entered the box, and a man's voice said 'Who's there?'

''Tis me, father,' I said for fear he mightn't see me and go away again. I couldn't see him at all. The place the voice came from was under the molding, about level with my knees, so I

---

[9]**molding**   piece of wood, plastic, stone, etc. which has been made into a
    particular shape to decorate the top or bottom of a wall, or a door, win-
    dow or piece of furniture (spelt 'moulding' in British English)

took a good grip of the molding and swung myself down till I saw the astonished face of a young priest looking up at me. He had to put his head on one side to see me, and I had to put mine on one side to see him, so we were more or less talking to one another upside-down. It struck me as a queer way of hearing confessions, but I didn't feel it my place to criticize.

'Bless me, father, for I have sinned; this is my first confession,' I rattled off all in one breath, and swung myself down the least shade more to make it easier for him.

'What are you doing up there?' he shouted in an angry voice, and the strain the politeness was putting on my hold of the molding, and the shock of being addressed in such an uncivil tone, were too much for me. I lost my grip, tumbled, and hit the door an unmerciful wallop before I found myself flat on my back in the middle of the aisle. The people who had been waiting stood up with their mouths open. The priest opened the door of the middle box and came out, pushing his biretta back from his forehead; he looked something terrible. Then Nora came scampering down the aisle.

'Oh, you dirty little caffler!' she said. 'I might have known you'd do it. I might have known you'd disgrace me. I can't leave you out of my sight for one minute.'

Before I could even get to my feet to defend myself she bent down and gave me a clip across the ear. This reminded me that I was so stunned I had even forgotten to cry, so that people might think I wasn't hurt at all, when in fact I was probably maimed for life. I gave a roar out of me.

'What's all this about?' the priest hissed, getting angrier than ever and pushing Nora off me. 'How dare you hit the child like that, you little vixen?'

'But I can't do my penance with him, father,' Nora cried, cocking an outraged eye up at him.

'Well, go and do it, or I'll give you some more to do,' he said, giving me a hand up. 'Was it coming to Confession you were, my poor man?' he asked me.

''Twas, father,' said I with a sob.

'Oh,' he said respectfully, 'a big hefty fellow like you must have terrible sins. Is this your first?'

''Tis, father,' said I.

'Worse and worse,' he said gloomily. 'The crimes of a life-time. I don't know will I get rid of you at all today. You'd better wait now till I'm finished with these old ones. You can see by the looks of them they haven't much to tell.'

'I will, father,' I said with something approaching joy.

The relief of it was really enormous. Nora stuck out her tongue at me from behind his back, but I couldn't even be bothered retorting. I knew from the very moment that man opened his mouth that he was intelligent above the ordinary. When I had time to think, I saw how right I was. It only stood to reason that a fellow confessing after seven years would have more to tell than people that went every week. The crimes of a lifetime, exactly as he said. It was only what he expected, and the rest was the cackle of old women and girls with their talk of Hell, the Bishop, and the penitential psalms. That was all they knew. I started to make my examination of conscience, and barring the one bad business of my grandmother it didn't seem so bad.

The next time, the priest steered me into the confession box himself and left the shutter back the way I could see him get in and sit down at the further side of the grille from me. 'Well, now,' he said, 'what do they call you?'

'Jackie, father,' said I.

'And what's a-trouble to you, Jackie?'

'Father,' I said, feeling I might as well get it over while I had him in good humor, 'I had it all arranged to kill my grand-mother.'

He seemed a bit shaken by that, all right, because he said nothing for quite a while.

'My goodness,' he said at last, 'that'd be a shocking thing to do. What put that into your head?'

'Father,' I said, feeling very sorry for myself, 'she's an awful woman.'

'Is she?' he asked. 'What way is she awful?'

'She takes porter, father,' I said, knowing well from the way Mother talked of it that this was a mortal sin, and hoping it would make the priest take a more favorable view of my case.

'Oh, my!' he said, and I could see he was impressed.

'And snuff, father,' said I.

'That's a bad case, sure enough, Jackie,' he said.

'And she goes round in her bare feet, father,' I went on in a rush of self-pity, 'and she knows I don't like her, and she gives pennies to Nora and none to me, and my da sides with her and flakes me, and one night I was so heart-scalded I made up my mind I'd have to kill her.'

'And what would you do with the body?' he asked with great interest.

'I was thinking I could chop that up and carry it away in a barrow I have,' I said.

'Begor, Jackie,' he said, 'do you know you're a terrible child?'

'I know, father,' I said, for I was just thinking the same thing myself. 'I tried to kill Nora too with a bread-knife under the table, only I missed her.'

'Is that the little girl that was beating you just now?' he asked.

''Tis, father.'

'Someone will go for her with a bread-knife one day, and he won't miss her,' he said rather cryptically. 'You must have great courage. Between ourselves, there's a lot of people I'd like to do the same to but I'd never have the nerve. Hanging is an awful death.'

'Is it, father?' I asked with the deepest interest – I was always very keen on hanging. 'Did you ever see a fellow hanged?'

'Dozens of them,' he said solemnly. 'And they all died roaring.'

'Jay!' I said.

'Oh, a horrible death!' he said with great satisfaction. 'Lots of the fellows I saw killed their grandmothers too, but they all said 'twas never worth it.'

He had me there for a full ten minutes talking, and then walked out the chapel yard with me. I was genuinely sorry to part with him, because he was the most entertaining character I'd ever met in the religious line. Outside, after the shadow of the church, the sunlight was like the roaring of waves on a beach; it dazzled me; and when the frozen silence melted and I heard the screech of trams on the road my heart soared. I knew now I wouldn't die in the night and come back, leaving marks on my mother's furniture. It would be a great worry to her, and the poor soul had enough.

Nora was sitting on the railing, waiting for me, and she put on a very sour puss when she saw the priest with me. She was mad jealous because a priest had never come out of the church with her.

'Well,' she asked coldly, after he left me, 'what did he give you?'

'Three Hail Marys,'[10] I said.

'Three Hail Marys,' she repeated incredulously. 'You mustn't have told him anything.'

'I told him everything,' I said confidently.

'About Gran and all?'

'About Gran and all.'

(All she wanted was to be able to go home and say I'd made a bad confession.)

'Did you tell him you went for me with the bread-knife?' she asked with a frown.

'I did to be sure.'

'And he only gave you three Hail Marys?'

'That's all.'

She slowly got down from the railing with a baffled air. Clearly, this was beyond her. As we mounted the steps back to the main road she looked at me suspiciously.

'What are you sucking?' she asked.

'Bullseyes.'

'Was it the priest gave them to you?'

---

[10]**Hail Marys**   a Catholic prayer to Mary, the mother of Jesus Christ

''Twas.'

'Lord God,' she wailed bitterly, 'some people have all the luck! 'Tis no advantage to anybody trying to be good. I might just as well be a sinner like you.'

Further reading

Another good Irish author for teenagers is Malachy Doyle. Look out for *Georgie* (Bloomsbury, 2004) and *Who Is Jesse Flood?* (Bloomsbury, 2002). The first book is a hard-hitting story about a boy who's so damaged that he attacks anyone and anything in sight. It is based on the author's experiences of working in special schools. The second book is based on his memories of being a teenager and focuses on a teenager's experience of trying to fit in with his peers. You can find more information on them at http://www.malachydoyle.co.uk/mdpage2c.html

Two texts about jumbies (Guyana)

by Grace Nichols

Guyana is the third-smallest country on the mainland of South America; it is approximately the size of Great Britain. Though geographically part of South America, culturally Guyana is Caribbean rather than Latin American and it is considered part of the West Indies. Superstition is a traditional part of the culture. In these texts, the well-known writer Grace Nichols remembers the stories of jumbies (ghosts or spirits) she was told during her childhood in Guyana.

I Like to Stay Up

I like to stay up
and listen
when big people talking
jumbie stories

I does feel
so tingly and excited
inside me

But when my mother say
'Girl, time for bed'

Then is when
I does feel a dread

Then is when
I does cover up
from me feet to me head

Then is when
I does wish I didn't listen
to no stupid jumbie story

Then is when
I does wish I did read
me book instead

Whole of a Morning Sky

On moonlight nights your room pale, like just before morning. At times you're tricked by it, thinking it almost morning, but then you always remember.

You remember him out there too. Standing with his legs astride the road. Tall-tall, with his throwback head gazing up at the moon. Head almost touching the moon. But only a fool would try to pass between his legs. Only a fool who want to die would try to slip past between them and give him the chance of snapping his legs together, crushing them flatter than a bake. That was the moongazer for you.

And outside you know the water is a smooth silvery plain. You could see her, the fair maid, combing the strands of her long hair with her comb of pure gold. If she drop the comb, as they're always doing, and if you happen to find it next morning then you have the chance of becoming the richest person on earth, because she'll give you anything to get it back. Anything.

Jumbies, on the other hand, like dark night so you have to be careful about that too. Like if you're coming home late one night and a jumbie following you (you know this from the swelling in your head), you mustn't go through your door backing him. Turn around and walk in back to front, facing him, giving a long suck teeth. Jumbies don't like kindness. You have to curse them and tell them 'bout their rotten navel. You know because your mother treated a jumbie kindly once and nearly died for it.

That was years ago when she was getting you. She told you the story many times. You were nearly not born.

It was an afternoon around sixish when darkness was just beginning to come. Your mother was between two minds. Whether to use the toilet bucket in her bedroom or to go all the way down to the pit latrine[1] which was right at the back of the yard, behind the school.

As it was still fairly light she decided to use the latrine and walked slowly down with her round heavy belly. But even before

---

[1]**pit latrine**   simple toilet consisting of a hole in the ground

she got there she could see that the door of the latrine was half open. But she didn't take it for anything and when she got there she was just about to push the door right back and step inside when she saw this old East Indian man, all dressed in his white dhoti,[2] sitting on the seat.

She was embarrassed and pulled back the door very quickly, saying, 'Goodnight, Oh, I'm very sorry.' Then she turned and began to make her way quickly to the house, because the strangest feeling was coming over her, as if she was being stifled by tobacco fumes. And suddenly she remembered that the man sitting on the latrine had no feet. After that she knew nothing more. It was Dinah who found her, lying near the foot of the steps in a dead faint.

When the Highdam people heard about it next day they quarrel with her for being so stupid. A woman expecting had to be extra careful. Evil spirits were always on the lookout for a new body to enter. She should have cursed the old wretch stinking.

And Aunt May make you feel frighten about losing your shadow. People have three shadows, she say. A long one, a medium-size one and a short one. Evil people could trap one of your shadows, making you get sick, keeping it until you got finer and finer, like a stick, until you died.

Further reading

If you enjoyed reading about jumbies, you might like to find out about the modern Western equivalent of such oral tales – the urban myth. You might have heard some of these yourself – the kind of fantastical stories that friends tell you that begin 'This amazing thing happened to my friend's friend . . . ' These tales get passed on from person to person and often change slightly from teller to teller. You could try *Now! That's What I Call Urban Myths* by Phil Healey and Rick Glanvill (Virgin Books, 1996).

---

[2]**dhoti**   loose clothing worn wrapped around the lower part of the body by men in India

Night of the Scorpion (India)

by Nissim Ezekiel

> In this poem, the narrator describes a frightening event in his child-
> hood – his mother is stung by a scorpion. Concerned neighbours
> visit her hut to help her and all sorts of cures are tried. Through his
> description of the event, the poet explores the cultural importance of
> superstition in India and also conveys his feelings about his mother.

I remember the night my mother
was stung by a scorpion. Ten hours
of steady rain had driven him
to crawl beneath a sack of rice.
Parting with his poison – flash
of diabolic[1] tail in the dark room –
he risked the rain again.
The peasants came like swarms of flies
and buzzed the Name of God a hundred times
to paralyse the Evil One.
With candles and with lanterns
throwing giant scorpion shadows
on the mud-baked walls
they searched for him: he was not found.
They clicked their tongues.
With every movement that the scorpion made
his poison moved in Mother's blood, they said.
May he sit still, they said.
May the sins of your previous birth
be burned away tonight, they said.
May your suffering decrease
the misfortunes of your next birth, they said.
May the sun of evil
balanced in this unreal world

---

[1]**diabolic**   devilish

against the sun of good
become diminished by your pain.
May the poison purify your flesh
of desire, and your spirit of ambition,
they said, and they sat around
on the floor with my mother in the centre,
the peace of understanding on each face.
More candles, more lanterns, more neighbours,
more insects, and the endless rain.
My mother twisted through and through
groaning on a mat.
My father, sceptic,[2] rationalist,[3]
trying every curse and blessing,
powder, mixture, herb and hybrid.
He even poured a little paraffin
upon the bitten toe and put a match to it.
I watched the flame feeding on my mother.
I watched the holy man perform his rites
to tame the poison with an incantation.[4]
After twenty hours
it lost its sting.

My mother only said,
Thank God the scorpion picked on me
and spared my children.

---

[2]**sceptic**   a person who doubts the truth of an idea
[3]**rationalist**   a person who adopts the practice or principle that actions and
    opinions should be based on reason rather than on emotion or religion
[4]**incantation**   words that are believed to have a magical effect when spoken
    or sung

Further reading

If you would like to read more poetry that originates in India, try the writing of Sujata Bhatt. You can find some of her poems and hear her reading them at the Poetry Archive site: http://www.poetryarchive.org

The Long Trial (North Africa)
by Andrée Chedid

Like many of the other texts in this section, this story explores the role of religion in cultural identity. It is set in the home of a poor family in Egypt. It shows the division of roles between men and women in this family, and the lack of power the woman has against the impact of poverty and religion and in her role as a wife. The story ends by showing her growing strength, as she defends her family against local traditions, with a shocking ending to the tale. This story was translated into English by David K. Bruner.

Someone was scratching at the door. Amina put her last nursling[1] on the ground and got up. Left alone, the little one shook with rage while one of his young sisters – half naked, moving on all fours – hurried towards him.

All at once the baby girl stopped still; fascinated by the tiny face of her younger brother, by his reddened cheeks and forehead. She probed his fragile eyelids, squashed with her index finger one of the baby's tears and carried it to her own mouth to taste the salt. Then she broke out sobbing, covering with her cries the wailing of the baby.

At the other end of the room – tiny, with mud walls and a low ceiling – which constituted the entire dwelling, two older children, their clothes in tatters, their hair straggling, their lips covered with flies, were beating upon each other for possession of a melon rind. Samyra, a seven-year-old, armed with a soup ladle, was chasing the chickens which scattered every which way. Her younger brother, Osman, was struggling to climb upon the back of a capering goat.

Before opening the door, Amina turned, annoyed, towards her string of children: 'Be quiet! If you wake your father, he'll beat the lot of you.' Her threats were in vain; among the nine children there were always some engaged in

---

[1]**nursling** baby

complaining or crying. She shrugged her shoulders and prepared to draw the bolt.

'Who knocked?' the sleepy voice of Zekr, her husband, asked.

It was the hour when the men dozed in their huts, those hardened and cracked cubes of mud, before returning to the fields. But the women, they remained watchful, always.

Amina disengaged the bolt from its cradle – the unscrewed crampons[2] held poorly to the wood – the hinges grated, making her gnash her teeth. How many times had she asked Zekr to oil those hinges! She pulled back the door and cried with joy:

'It's Hadj Osman!'

Hadj Osman had several times made the holy pilgrimage to Mecca; his virtue was widely known. For many years he had wandered about the country, begging his bread and freely giving his blessings. When he passed by, maladies[3] disappeared, the growing crops took on a new vigour. Villagers recognized him from a great distance by his long black robe, topped with a sash of khaki wool with which he wrapped his chest and head.

'You honour our house, holy man. Enter!'

At a single visit prayers were answered. One told that at the village of Suwef, thanks to the putting on of hands, a young man who had made only throat sounds since birth was suddenly made to articulate.[4] Amina had herself been witness to the miracle of Zeinab, a girl just at puberty who terrified her neighbours with her frequent fits – rolling about in the sand, her legs wild and her lip pulled up. Hadj Osman was called in; he said a few words; ever since that time Zeinab had remained calm. One was even speaking now of finding a husband for her.

Amina opened the door more widely. Light inundated[5] the room.

'Enter, holy man. Our home is your home.'

---

[2]**crampons** metal studs
[3]**maladies** illnesses
[4]**articulate** speak
[5]**inundated** flooded

The man excused himself, preferring to remain outside.

'Bring me some bread and water. I have made a long journey; my strength has left me.'

Awake with a start, Zekr recognized the voice. He hastened to put on his calotte[6] and, grasping the water jug by the handle, he got up, bleary, advanced rubbing his eyes.

When her husband reached the threshold and saluted the old man, the woman retired.

The door closed, Amina turned toward her stove of pressed earth. No amount of fatigue could bend her back. She had that sovereign carriage of Egyptian peasants which makes the head seem always to balance and carry a fragile and heavy burden.

Was she young? Hardly thirty! But what good is youth, if no care is taken for it?

At the stove, the woman leaned forward to draw from a nook the bread for the week, rolled in jute[7] cloth. A few dried olives lying in a bowl, two strings of onions hanging on the wall. The woman counted the flatcakes, hefted[8] them; she placed them against her cheek to test their freshness. Having chosen the two best, she dusted them with the back of her sleeve, blew upon them. Then, taking them as an offering, between her open hands, she advanced again to the door.

The presence of the visitor delighted her. Her hut seemed less wretched, her children less squalling, and the voice of Zekr more lively, more animated.

On the way she bumped into two of her children. One hung upon her skirts, stretching up to seize a flatcake:

'Give me. I'm hungry.'

'Go away, Barsoum. It's not for you. Let go!'

'I'm not Barsoum. I'm Ahmed.'

The darkness of the room obscured their faces.

---

[6]**calotte**   a plain religious skull cap
[7]**jute**   fibre used for making rope and cloth
[8]**hefted**   picked up and weighed in her hands

'I'm hungry!'

She shoved him back. The child slipped, fell, rolled upon the earth and howled.

Feeling herself at fault, she hastened forward, pushed the door open quickly, crossed the threshold. She closed the door immediately and leaned back against it with all her weight. Her face sweaty, her mouth pressed shut, she stood motionless, facing the old man and her husband, and drew breath deeply into her lungs.

'The eucalyptus[9] under which I repose,[10] which grows in the midst of a field of oats . . .' began Hadj Osman.

'It is still there,' sighed the woman.

'The last time, it seemed very sickly.'

'It's still there,' she replied. 'Here, nothing ever changes. Nothing at all.'

What she had just said gave her a sudden wish to cry and to complain. The old man could hear her; he might console her, perhaps? But for what? She didn't know exactly. 'For everything' she thought to herself.

'Take these cakes. They are for you!'

The empty water jug lay upon the ground. Hadj Osman took the flatcakes from the hands of the woman and thanked her. He slipped one of the cakes between his robe and the skin of his chest; he bit into the other. He chewed diligently, making each mouthful last a long time.

Pleased to see him regain strength because of her bread, Amina smiled once again. Then, remembering that her husband objected severely to her remaining any length of time outside the house, she took leave of the two men, bowing to them.

'May Allah heap blessings upon you!' the old man exclaimed. 'May he bless you and grant you seven more children!'

The woman pressed against the wall to keep from staggering, she shrank into her large, black clothing, she hid her face.

---

[9]**eucalyptus**   a type of tree
[10]**repose**   lie down

'What's the matter? Are you ill?' the old man asked.

She was unable to form the words. At last she blurted out:

'I have nine children already, holy man, I beg you withdraw your benediction.'[11]

He thought he must have misunderstood; she articulated so poorly:

'What did you say? Repeat.'

'Take back your benediction, I beg you.'

'I don't understand you,' interrupted the old man. 'You don't know what you are saying.'

Her face still buried in her hands, the woman shook her head from right to left, from left to right:

'No! No! . . . Enough! . . . It is enough!'

All around children metamorphosed[12] into grasshoppers, bounded against her, encircled her, transformed her into a clod of earth, inert. Their hundreds of hands became claws, nettles twitching her clothes, tearing her flesh.

'No! No! . . . I can't endure any more!'

She choked:

'Take back the benediction!'

Zekr, petrified by her aplomb,[13] stood facing her, not opening his mouth.

'The benedictions come from the hand of God, I can change nothing in them.'

'You can . . . You *must* take them back!'

With a smirk of disdain, Hadj Osman turned his head away.

But she continued to harass him:

'Take back the benediction! Speak to me. You must take back the benediction.'

She clenched her fists and advanced towards him:

'You must reply to me!'

The old man pushed her back with both hands:

---

[11]**benediction**   blessing
[12]**metamorphosed**   transformed
[13]**aplomb**   self-confidence

'Nothing. I withdraw nothing.'

She reared, advanced again. Was she the same woman of but a few moments ago?

'Take back the benediction,' she hurled.

From what source had she got that look, that voice?

'What use is it to tame the waters? What good are the promised harvests? Here, everywhere there will be thousands of other mouths to feed! Have you looked at our children? What do they look like to you! If you only looked at them!'

Opening wide the door of her hovel, she called in:

'Barsoum, Fatma, Osman, Naghi! Come. Come, all of you. The bigger ones carry the smaller ones in their arms. Come out, all nine. Show yourselves!'

'You are mad!'

'Show your arms, your shoulders! Lift your dress, show your stomachs, your thighs, your knees!'

'You deny life!' the old man sneered.

'Don't talk to me about life! You know nothing about life!'

'Children – they are life!'

'Too many children – they are death!'

'Amina, you blaspheme!'[14]

'I call upon God!'

'God will not hear you.'

'He will hear me!'

'If I were your husband, I'd chastize you.'

'No one, today, no one will lift a hand to me. No one!' She seized the moving arm of Hadj Osman:

'Not even you! . . . Take back the benediction or I will not let loose.'

She shook him to force him to recall his words:

'Do what I tell you: take back the benediction!'

'You are possessed! Get back; don't touch me again. I withdraw nothing!'

---

[14]**blaspheme**   swear or use words that are disrespectful to religion and God

Even though the old man had several times called upon him to speak, Zekr remained mute and immobile. Then, brusquely, he moved. Would he hurl himself upon Amina and beat her, as he usually did?

'You, Zekr, on your knees! Now you! You make him understand. Beg him! With me.'

The words had come from her! How had she dared to say them? and with such an imperious[15] tone? Suddenly, seized with a trembling, strangled with old fears, she unclenched her fists; her limbs grew soft as cotton. Elbows raised to protect herself from blows, she shrivelled against the wall.

'The woman is right, holy man. Take back the benediction.'

She couldn't believe her ears. Nor her eyes. Zekr had heard her. Zekr was there on his knees at the feet of the old man.

Alerted by the clamour, neighbours came running in from all sides. Zekr sought the eye of Amina kneeling beside him; the woman was overwhelmed with gratitude.

'Holy man, take back the benediction,' the two implored[16] together.

A tight circle formed about them. Feeling himself supported by that crowd, the old man stretched up on his toes and raised a menacing index finger:

'This man, this woman reject the work of God. They sin! Drive them out. Else an evil will fall upon the village!'

'Seven children! He has ordained[17] seven more children upon us! What can we do?' groaned Amina.

Fatma, her cousin, already had eight. Soad, six. Fathia, who always accompanied her younger sister of the rotten teeth and the wild eyes, had four sons and three daughters. And the others? It was the same story . . . Yet, each of the women, fearful, hesitant, looked mistrustfully at Amina.

---

[15]**imperious**   proud
[16]**implored**   begged
[17]**ordained**   ordered

'Births are in God's hands,' said Fatma, seeking the approbation of the old man – and of the other men.

'It's up to us to decide whether we want children,' proclaimed Zekr, leaping up.

'That's blasphemy,' protested Khalifé, a young man with protruding ears. 'Something bad will happen to us!'

'Drive them out!' the old man insisted. 'They profane[18] the place.'

Amina put her hand fraternally upon her husband's shoulder.

'We must listen to Hadj Osman; he's a holy man,' murmured a few disturbed voices.

'No, it is I you must listen to!' cried Zekr, 'I who am like all of you. It's Amina you must listen to, Amina who is a woman like other women. How could she bear seven more children? What could we do?'

His cheeks were aflame. From way back someone made a timid echo:

'What will they do?'

From mouth to mouth those words swelled:

'What will they do?'

'No more children!' suddenly uttered a blind little girl clinging to her mother's skirts.

What was happening to this village, to these people, to this valley? Hadj Osman sadly shook his head.

'No more children!' the voices repeated.

Swinging between his crutches, Mahmoud, the one-legged, approached the old man and whispered to him:

'Take back your benediction.'

'I withdraw nothing!'

Pushing with his elbows to disengage himself from the crowd, the holy man spat out curses; and with an angry motion he upset the cripple, who lost hold of his crutches and rolled to the ground.

That was the signal.

Fikhry threw himself upon the old man. To avenge the one-legged man, Zekr struck also. Salah, whipping the air with his

---
[18]**profane**   show no respect for God or religion

bamboo cane, approached. It was a sarabande of motion and cries. Hoda ran in with a piece of garden hose. A little boy pulled up a boundary stake. An elderly man broke a branch from a weeping willow and entered into the melee.[19]

'No more children!'
'Take back your benediction!'
'We won't endure any more!'
'We want to live.'
'Live!'

Towards evening the police found Hadj Osman stretched out, face down, next to a trampled flatcake and a water jug broken into bits. They raised him up, brushed off his garments, and took him to the nearest dispensary.[20]

The next day, a police raid took place in the village. The men who had taken part in the melee were driven off in a paddy wagon. The vehicle bounced off, down the long tow-path which led to the police station.

Eyes shining, Amina and her companions gathered at the edge of the village, stared a long while down the road. Clouds of dust rose and spread.

Their husbands weren't really going away, leaving them behind . . . never had they felt themselves so close together. Never.

That day was not a day like all other days.

That day, the long trial had reached its end.

Further reading

Another writer who often considers the roles of men and women in his poetry is Benjamin Zephaniah. Look out for his poems *Man to Man* and *Miss World*. You can find the text of *Man to Man* at http://www.britishcouncil.org/zephaniah_activity5-2.pdf. You can hear *Miss World* at

http://www.bbc.co.uk/arts/poetry/outloud/zephaniah.shtml.

---

[19]**melee**   disorganised fight
[20]**dispensary**   medical centre

The Storyteller's Daughter
(Afghanistan/England)
by Saira Shah

This extract is from a book by a female journalist of Afghan descent but brought up in England. While she experienced childhood as an English girl, she learned about her Afghan heritage from the many stories her father told her. She is a woman who thinks of herself as half Afghan warrior and half Western liberal and feels loyalty to both cultures. The book documents her travels, as a Western woman journalist, in dangerous areas of Afghanistan during the time of the Soviet invasion of that country. It is a book about courage, strength and the richness of learning from other people and cultures.

I am three years old. I am sitting on my father's knee. He is telling me of a magical place: the fairytale landscape you enter in dreams. Fountains fling diamond droplets into mosaic pools. Coloured birds sing in the fruit-laden orchards. The pomegranates burst and their insides are rubies. Fruit is so abundant that even the goats are fed on melons. The water has magical properties: you can fill to bursting with fragrant *pilau*,[1] then step to the brook and drink – and you will be ready to eat another meal.

On three sides of the plateau majestic mountains tower, capped with snow. The fourth side overlooks a sunny valley where, gleaming far below, sprawls a city of villas and minarets.[2] And here is the best part of the story: it is true.

The garden is in Paghman, where my family had its seat for nine hundred years. The jewel-like city it overlooks is the Afghan capital, Kabul. The people of Paghman call the capital Kabul *jan*: beloved Kabul. We call it that too, for this is where we belong.

---

[1] *pilau*   rice cooked in a spicy liquid
[2] **minaret**   tall thin tower on or near a mosque from which Muslims are called to pray

'Whatever outside appearances may be, no matter who tells you otherwise, this garden, this country, these are your origin. This is where you are truly from. Keep it in your heart, Saira *jan*. Never forget.'

Any Western adult might have told me that this was an exile's[3] tale of a lost Eden: the place you dream about, to which you can never return. But even then, I wasn't going to accept that. Even then, I had absorbed enough of the East to feel I belonged there. And too much of the West not to try to nail down dreams.

My father understood the value of stories: he was a writer. My parents had picked Kent as an idyllic place to bring up their children, but we were never allowed to forget our Afghan background.

Periodically during my childhood, my father would come upon the kitchen like a storm. Western systematic method quickly melted before the inspiration of the East. Spice jars tumbled down from their neat beech-wood rack and disgorged heaps of coloured powder on to the melamine sideboard. Every pan was pressed into service and extra ones were borrowed from friends and neighbours. The staid old Aga[4] wheezed exotic vapours – *saffran, zeera, gashneesh*;[5] their scents to this day are as familiar to me as my own breath.

In the midst of this mayhem[6] presided[7] my father, the alchemist. Like so many expatriates,[8] when it came to maintaining the traditions, customs and food of his own country he was *plus royaliste que le roi*.[9] Rather than converting lead into

---

[3]**exile**   someone sent or kept away from their own country for political reasons
[4]**Aga**   a large iron cooker which keeps its heat
[5]*saffran, zeera, gashneesh*   spices
[6]**mayhem**   chaos
[7]**presided**   ruled
[8]**expatriates**   people who do not live in their own country
[9]*plus royaliste que le roi*   more royalist than the king

gold, my father's alchemical art transported our English country kitchen to the furthest reaches of the Hindu Kush.[10]

We children were the sorcerer's apprentices: we chopped onions and split cardamom[11] pods, nibbling the fragrant black seeds as we worked. We crushed garlic and we peeled tomatoes. He showed us how to steep saffron, to strain yoghurt and to cook the rice until it was *dana-dar*, possessing grains – that is, to the point where it crumbles into three or four perfect round seeds if you rub it between your fingers.

In the kitchen, my father's essential *Afghaniyat*, Afghan-ness, was most apparent. The Afghan love of *pilau* is as fundamental to the national character as the Italian fondness for spaghetti. The Amir Habibullah, a former ruler of Afghanistan, would demolish a vast meal of *pilau*, meatballs and sauce for lunch, then turn to his courtiers and ask: 'Now, noblemen and friends, what shall we cook tonight?'

We knew to produce at least three times more *pilau* than anyone could ever be expected to eat. Less would have been an insult to our name and contrary to the Afghan character. As my great-great-great-grandfather famously roared: 'How dare you ask me for a *small* favour?'

If, at any point, my father found himself with an unexpected disaster – rice that went soggy or an over-boiling pan that turned the Aga's hotplate into a sticky mess – he would exclaim: 'Back in Afghanistan, we had cooks to do this work!'

He would tell us, with Afghan hyperbole: 'We are making a *Shahi pilau*, a *pilau* fit for kings. This recipe has been handed down through our family since it was prepared for up to four thousand guests at the court of your ancestors. It is far better than the *pilau* you will find when you visit homes in Afghanistan today.'

On one notable occasion, my father discovered the artificial food colouring, tartrazine. A *pilau*-making session was

---

[10]**Hindu Kush**   mountain range in Afghanistan
[11]**cardamom**   an Indian spice

instantly convened. Like a conjurer pulling off a particularly effective trick, he showed us how just one tiny teaspoon could transform a gigantic cauldron of *pilau* to a virulent shade of yellow. We were suitably impressed. From that moment on, traditional saffron was discarded for this intoxicating substance.

Years later, I learned that all of the Afghan dishes my father had taught me diverged[12] subtly from their originals. His method of finishing off the parboiled rice in the oven, for example, was an innovation of his own. Straining yoghurt through cheesecloth turned out to be merely the first stage in an elaborate process. In Kent, rancid[13] sheep's fat was hard to come by, so he substituted butter. Cumin[14] was an Indian contamination.[15] And so it went on.

Yet although his methods and even his ingredients were different, my father's finished dishes tasted indistinguishable from the originals. He had conveyed their essential quality; the minutiae had been swept away.

During these cookery sessions, we played a wonderful game. We planned the family trip to Afghanistan that always seemed to be just round the corner. How we would go back to Paghman, stroll in the gardens, visit our old family home and greet the relatives we had never met. When we arrived in the Paghman mountains, the men would fire their guns in the air – we shouldn't worry, that was the Afghan way of welcome and celebration. They would carry us on their shoulders, whooping and cheering, and in the evening we would eat a *pilau* that eclipsed even the great feasts of the court of our ancestors.

My mother's family background, which is Parsee[16] from India, rarely got a look in. As far as my father was concerned, his

---

[12]**diverged**   differed
[13]**rancid**   (of butter, oil, etc.) tasting or smelling unpleasant because not fresh
[14]**cumin**   a spice
[15]**contamination**   impurity
[16]**Parsee**   a member of a religious group found mainly in western India, whose religion, Zoroastrianism, started in Persia (ancient Iran)

offspring were pure Afghan. For years, the mere mention of the Return was enough to stoke us children into fits of excitement. It was so much more alluring than our mundane[17] Kentish lives, which revolved round the family's decrepit Land Rover and our pet labrador, Honey.

'Can we take the Land Rover?' asked my brother Tahir.

'We shall take a fleet of Land Rovers,' said my father grandly.

My sister Safia piped up: 'Can we take Honey?'

There was an uncomfortable pause. Even my father's flight of fantasy balked at introducing to Afghans as a beloved member of our family that unclean animal, the dog.

When I was fifteen, the Soviet Union invaded and occupied Afghanistan. During a *pilau*-making session quite soon after that, I voiced an anxiety that had been growing for some time now. How could my father expect us to be truly Afghan when we had grown up outside an Afghan community? When we went back home, wouldn't we children be strangers, foreigners in our own land? I expected, and possibly hoped for, the soothing account of our triumphant and imminent return to Paghman. It didn't come. My father looked tired and sad. His answer startled me: 'I've given you stories to replace a community. They are your community.'

'But surely stories can't replace experience.'

He picked up a packet of dehydrated onion. 'Stories are like these onions – like dried experience. They aren't the original experience but they are more than nothing at all. You think about a story, you turn it over in your mind, and it becomes something else.' He added hot water to the onion. 'It's not fresh onion – fresh experience – but it is something that can help you to recognize experience when you come across it. Experiences follow patterns, which repeat themselves again and again. In our tradition, stories can help you recognize the shape of an experience, to make sense of and to deal with it. So, you see, what you may take

---

[17]**mundane**   boring, everyday

for mere snippets of myth and legend encapsulate what you need to know to guide you on your way anywhere among Afghans.'

'Well, as soon as I'm eighteen I'm going to go to see for myself,' I said, adding craftily: 'Then perhaps I'll have fresh experiences that will help me grow up.'

My father had been swept along on the tide of his analogy.[18] Now, he suddenly became a parent whose daughter was at an impressionable age and whose country was embroiled in a murderous war.

'If you would only grow up a little in the first place,' he snapped, 'then you would realize that you don't need to go at all.'

April 2001
At thirty-six years old, I have never seen Afghanistan at peace. I am choking under the *burqa*,[19] the pale blue veil, which begins in a cap upon my head. It covers my face, my body, my arms and my legs, and is long enough to trip me up in my muddy plastic shoes. A crocheted grille obscures my vision. A grid of black shadows intersects trees, fields and the white road outside. It is like looking out through prison bars.

I have not had enough air for four hours now and we have eight more to go before we reach Kabul. I have an almost irresistible urge to do whatever it takes to breathe, simply breathe. How can I describe it? I want to rip off the *burqa* in the way that a drowning man will grapple his rescuer in his urge to reach the air above. But I cannot: it is all that protects me from the Taliban. Even lifting the front flap of my *burqa* is a crime, punishable by a beating.

---

[18]**analogy**   comparison between two things that have similar features
[19]***burqa***   an all-enveloping outer garment worn by most Muslim women in Afghanistan, and many in India and Pakistan. It is worn over the usual daily clothing and removed when the woman returns home. Before the Taliban took power in Afghanistan, it was little worn in cities. During the Taliban's reign, women were required to wear a *burqa* whenever they appeared in public. The full or Afghan *burqa* covers the wearer's entire face except for a small region about the eyes, which is covered by a concealing net or grille.

In the front of the car, the taxi driver fumbles in a secret compartment and produces a cassette. It is a good sign: music is banned. I was told that we would have a safe car with a driver we knew, but when it came down to it, we jumped into a taxi at random. If he is willing to play music in front of us, perhaps the taxi driver and we may trust each other. We are fellow conspirators. Perhaps he will not give us away.

Afghan popular music blares out, singing of lover and beloved. The Taliban detest this kind of language. The refrain goes, *Jan, jan . . .*' and I feel a sudden flash of happiness. It's crazy: in ten minutes, I could be dead. But I can't help myself. We are heading for Kabul – beloved Kabul.

On the face of it, I am a journalist, filming a documentary for Channel Four Television, called *Beneath the Veil* about the Taliban's Afghanistan. Now I have left my crew behind, to travel in disguise with the Revolutionary Association of the Women of Afghanistan.

We have just crossed the border illegally into Taliban-controlled Afghanistan. As a Westerner, if I am caught, I may be imprisoned and accused of espionage.[20] If the Taliban discover my family history and decide I am an Afghan, then I share the same risks as the Afghan women who are helping me: torture, a bullet in the head or simply disappearing in Puli Charki, Kabul's notorious political prison. The women are willing to take this risk because they belong to an organization that opposes the Taliban. Their activities – secret schools and clinics for women – are already politically subversive[21] enough to get them killed.

Beside me, my female companion is being sick. She holds a plastic bag, and vomits without lifting her *burqa*.

I don't need to ask her what she is doing here: I need to ask myself.

For many years, in the secret cubbyhole where precious things were stored, my father kept a dusty file containing two pieces of paper. The first was the crumbling title deed to our estate in Paghman. The other was our family tree, stretching back before the Prophet Muhammad, two thousand years back, to the time before my family had even heard of Afghanistan.

The title deed was no longer worth the paper it was written on. In Afghanistan, if you are not present to defend your property, you had better be prepared to take it back by the gun. As for our family tree, we didn't need a piece of paper to tell us who we were. My father, and his father before him, saw to it that our lineage was etched on our hearts.

Our family traces its descent through Fatima, the daughter of the Prophet Muhammad. The man who, during his lifetime, founded one of the world's great monotheistic religions,[22] who united the feuding tribes of Arabia, and who could have accumulated wealth beyond compare, died in poverty. On his deathbed he left this bequest:[23] 'I have nothing to leave you, except my family.' Since then, his descendants have been revered throughout the Muslim world. They are entitled to use the honorific Sayed.[24]

My grandfather maintained that ancestry was something to try to live up to, not to boast about. As an old man, his hooded, faintly Mongolian eyes, his hooked nose and his tall *karakul*[25] lambskin hat made him look like an inscrutable[26] sage[27] from a Mughal miniature. I remember this venerable figure telling me a joke: 'They asked a mule: "What kind of creature are you?" He replied: "Well, my mother was a horse!"'

The old man laughed, enjoying the punch-line, and so did I, though I barely understood it. 'Do you understand? He was only a mule, but he boasted of the horse, his ancestor! So, you

---

[22]**monotheistic religions**   religions based on belief in one god
[23]**bequest**   what a person leaves to others on their death
[24]**honorific Sayed**   a title that indicates lineage with the family of the Islamic prophet Muhammad
[25]*karakul*   a breed of domesticated sheep
[26]**inscrutable**   not showing emotions
[27]**sage**   wise man

see, Saira *jan*, it is less important who your forebears were than what you yourself become.'

Islam, as I absorbed it, was a tolerant[28] philosophy, which encouraged one to adopt a certain attitude to life. The Qur'an[29] we studied taught: 'There is no compulsion in religion.' The Prophet we followed said: 'The holy warrior is he who struggles with himself.'

Many of the sayings of the Prophet that I was raised on are from a compilation[30] by the Afghan authority Baghawi of Herat. In the orthodox Muslim world it is eclipsed[31] by the monumental collection of Imam Bokhari. Bokhari set out to preserve the literal words and traditions of the Prophet as an act of pious[32] scholasticism.[33] He investigated six hundred thousand sayings, passing only around five thousand as incontestably[34] authentic.[35]

The purpose of Baghawi's collection, on the other hand, is instrumental, rather than scholastic. It was revered by the classical Persian poets, and is widely used in dervish[36] mystical communities to this day. Sayings are included for content. The distinction between these two great Islamic figures is a matter of emphasis: the literal or the spiritual.

Probably because Afghans were thin on the ground in Tunbridge Wells, my father hired an Iranian Qur'an teacher for us. We didn't like him. He felt that, when it came to the Holy Word of God, rote learning[37] was more important than understanding. He

---

[28]**tolerant**   willing to accept beliefs or behaviour that are different from one's own

[29]**Qur'an**   the holy book of the Islamic religion

[30]**compilation**   collection

[31]**eclipsed**   overshadowed

[32]**pious**   holy

[33]**scholasticism**   emphasising traditional teachings by studying them in detail

[34]**incontestably**   definitely

[35]**authentic**   genuine

[36]**dervish**   a member of a Muslim religious group which has an energetic dance as part of its worship

[37]**rote learning**   learning by heart

slapped my six-year-old sister for failing to memorize in Arabic the mystical verse from the Qur'an known as the Niche for Lights:

Allah is the light of the heavens and of the earth.
His light is like a niche,[38] *wherein there is a lamp:*
The lamp within a glass, the glass like unto a pearly star.
It is lit from a blessed olive tree
Neither of the East, nor of the West
The oil of which itself shines, although fire has touched it not:
Light upon light!

Outside our sealed bubble of tolerant Muslim culture, the Islamic world was changing. Some years before the Iranian revolution, our Qur'an teacher became fascinated by the ideas of Ayatollah Khomeini.[39] He was hurriedly dismissed, and he eventually returned to Iran to study in a religious seminary.[40] When the thirst for Islamic revolution had stirred his heart sufficiently, he decided he had been brought to our household for a purpose: to witness the depravity[41] and error into which our branch of the family of the Prophet had sunk. For a while, we children were hurried past the thick laurel bushes in the driveway, in case our erstwhile[42] Qur'an instructor was lurking there, ready to attack us.

What unacceptable religious ideas had he encountered in our home? What teachings did he find so detrimental to the hearts of the faithful? Perhaps Baghawi of Herat's sayings of the Prophet, which adjured[43] one to think for oneself rather than conform to externals without question:

One hour's teaching is better than a whole night of prayer.
Trust in God, but tie your camel first.

---

[38]**niche** small hollow
[39]**Ayatollah Khomeini** a religious leader in Iran and considered by many Muslims as an influential spiritual thinker
[40]**seminary** a college for training religious people
[41]**depravity** moral evil
[42]**erstwhile** former
[43]**adjured** directed

The ink of the learned is holier than the blood of the martyr.
You ask me to curse unbelievers, but I was not sent to curse.
I order you to help any oppressed person, whether they are Muslim or not.
Women are the twin halves of men.

These were the values I grew up with. This was the Islam I bought into.

April 2001

Now I have entered a world where I am forbidden to show my face, paint my nails or fly a kite. Nothing is too trivial for the scholars of Islamic law to prohibit. Even paper bags are banned – just in case the paper they are composed of should chance to have written upon it the Holy Name of Allah, which might consequently run the risk of defilement.[44] Allah really cares about getting the details right. There is a serious debate raging as to whether the acceptable Islamic way to punish homosexuality is by tipping a wall over the offender, or by throwing him off the highest minaret.

Nothing is permitted unless the Holy Qur'an specifically sanctions it, or unless it is an authenticated[45] practice of the Prophet. Everything else must undergo examination by the religious scholars. They use a rigorous process of analogy and theological debate to determine what is permitted and what is prohibited. The Ministry for the Prevention of Vice and the Promotion of Virtue, the feared religious police, enforces their edicts.

The twenty-first century throws up constant challenges to faith. Television and video are banned, but cassette tape might contain Qur'anic recitations. It should only be destroyed if there is music on it. Instrumental music is not permitted, but simple religious chants are allowed.

Cigarettes are permitted, but some cigarette packets have pictures of women on them. These are banned. The strictest

---

[44]**defilement**   being spoilt or made dirty
[45]**authenticated**   proved to be true

care must be taken not to allow images of the human form. Passport photographs present a dilemma. It has been determined that the heads and shoulders of males may be shown, for the purpose of identification. Top-to-toe shots are unlawful.

The stakes are high: this is the prototype for a perfect Islamic state. Morals must be above reproach. Women must be protected, and the best way to do that is to keep them indoors. They are prohibited from going outside without a male relative as an escort. Even then, they must be entirely covered in the *burqa*, to prevent them leading men into temptation. Girls over nine are barred from school. Females are banned from almost all jobs.

Sufism, the philosophical tradition of my forebears, has been pushed underground. The Taliban deplore its assertion that spiritual essentials are more important than external practices.

My ancestors maintained that the Qur'an was revealed in seven layers, with an outer, literal meaning, and successive deeper levels of mystical value. Their suggestion that, while it is possible to rise by the Shariah, the religious law, the Prophet also had an inner circle of disciples to whom he taught an esoteric[46] path, is now regarded as heresy.[47]

The border post at the mouth of the Khyber Pass is controlled by Taliban guards. Through the *burqa*'s grille I see them patrolling. They wear the trademark black turbans of Kandahar, the hometown of their movement. We will have to cross the frontier on foot, under their gaze. Wearing the *burqa* is an art that I haven't had time to acquire, and I trip trying to clamber out of the car. I am aware that I walk too confidently: like a Westerner – or a man. I try to look suitably submissive. I hunch my shoulders and attempt to efface even my thoughts.

There are three of us. A man and a woman alone might excite suspicion: the Taliban might demand proof that we are

---

[46]**esoteric**   linked to specialist knowledge
[47]**heresy**   a belief that is against the mainstream

married or related. But one man with two veiled women, following a few footsteps behind, is too common a sight to arouse suspicion.

I have rehearsed my cover story and learned off pat the answers I will give if I am stopped and questioned. My name is Fatima. I come from the southern town of Ghazni. I am an Afghan refugee, returning to visit my family in Kabul for my sister's wedding. I am Persian-speaking. I do not speak Pushtu, the language of the Taliban.

But nobody stops me. The Taliban guards neither smile nor scowl as we pass. They do not even look at me. I require no documents. I am merely a notation on the papers of my male escort. As a woman, I have ceased to exist. The *burqa* is my passport, my cloak of invisibility.

It occurs to me that I have been doing this all my life: using the raw materials of a culture to subvert it. Although I have spent my adult life chasing the dream of a national identity, my allegiance is not to a country, or even to a tribe. It is to a set of values.

Two people live inside me. Like a couple who rarely speak, they are not compatible. My Western side is a sensitive, liberal, middle-class pacifist. My Afghan side I can only describe as a rapacious robber baron. It revels in bloodshed, glories in risk and will not be afraid.

In 1842, nearly five thousand fighting men – the whole Kabul force of the British army – were hacked to pieces by an Afghan horde. Twelve thousand camp followers – unarmed and innocent civilians – were also butchered. Only one man made it to safety. The exhausted Dr Brydon, humiliatingly mounted on a donkey, was the sole surviving representative of Afghanistan's British occupiers. His arrival brought tidings to a stunned world that an entire British army had been wiped out. This human catastrophe inspired a gloating Afghan battle song:

Doktor brydon, khar-i lang-ash
Ham quwad dar khak-i mast

Doctor Brydon, on his lame donkey,
All his troops are in our soil.

I grew up applauding a massacre that, if it happened today, I would surely condemn as an atrocity. The song has a catchy tune and I used to hum it during netball practice at my grammar school. I didn't mean anything by it politically: I was oblivious to the irony of my situation. However, if British identity can be judged by which team you support, I suppose I failed the test.

My own identity was shaped more by myths and legends than by my passport or birth certificate. Most of them enshrined lessons from history.

Further reading

Another interesting book about mixed race experience is Doris Pilkington's *Rabbit-proof Fence* (Miramax Books, 2002). The true story traces the journey home of three girls taken from their community in Northwestern Australia. Following a government edict in 1931, black children and children of mixed marriages were taken to settlements where they were taught to abandon their aboriginal heritage and become culturally white. The girls escape from the Moore River Native Settlement and walk 1500 miles back to their family. Like Saira Shah's book, their story focuses on human strength and resilience.

If you want to read more about Afghanistan, *My Forbidden Face* (Virago, 2002) by Latifa is a true story written by a 16-year-old girl. After Afghanistan was taken over by the Taliban, she recorded events as they happened to her and her family over a five-year period.

Activities

Film Boy

Before you read

1   Think about someone famous whom you could consider a personal hero.
    ● Why do you admire them?
    ● If you met them, what three questions would you like to ask them?

Share your answers with the rest of your class.

What's it about?

Read the story and write down your answers to questions 2 and 3.

2   Read the first section of the story (up to 'something he would like very much indeed') again, focusing on the character of Prem. What do you learn about his character? List four things; use quotations from the story to support each point.

3   What do we learn about the life of a successful Bollywood film star from the descriptions of Rasi's home and lifestyle?

Thinking about the text

4   a   The author portrays the guard as unpleasant, rather than as a man just doing his job. Pick out two phrases in this story that suggest this and comment on their effect.

    b   Look carefully at the paragraphs describing Prem's escape from the guard (from 'Thief!' to 'a desk near the window', page 178). How does the author create a sense of fear and tension through his use of language? Use evidence from the text to support your answer.

5   Find out more about the genre of Bollywood films.
    ● What features would you expect to find in this genre of film?
    ● How do they differ from modern Hollywood or British films?

Discuss your findings with the rest of your class.

6   Prepare a three-minute informative presentation to the class on a personal hero. Include facts about this person's life as well as two or three anecdotes to interest your listeners. You might like to use music or images to illustrate your talk.

First Confession

Before you read

1   What is 'guilt'? Working with a partner, write your own definition. Then think of a time when you have felt very guilty in your life. Share your anecdote with your partner.

2   Do you know any of the ten commandments of Christianity? These are rules for living a Christian life as laid down in the Bible. As a class, see how many of them you know.

What's it about?

Read the text and answer questions 3 to 5 by yourself. Then compare your answers with a partner's.

3   Look carefully at the first line of the story. What does the language suggest about the story to come? Do you think it is a good opening to a story? Give reasons for your answer.

4   What effect does the character Mrs Ryan have on Jackie's childish mind? How do you know this from what he tells us?

5   What impression does the narrator give us of his sister on page 188? Do you think what he tells us is all true and reliable?

Thinking about the text

6   What is your opinion of the actions of the priest? Working with a partner, improvise a discussion between the priest and Nora in which she asks him to explain his behaviour.

7   In this story Frank O'Connor takes a rather humorous perspective on religion, childhood and a child's view of religious rituals. Working in a small group, skim the text and identify sections of the text that are humorous.

8   This story focuses on an important ceremony in a Catholic child's life – his or her first Confession. Think of a turning point or important event in your own life and write a descriptive piece to help your reader imagine the event and understand its importance.

Two texts about jumbies

Before you read

1   *Whole of a Morning Sky* mentions various mythical characters of childhood – the water maiden and the moongazer. Can you think of any traditional, mythical childhood characters from your own culture? Share your memories with a partner.

What's it about?

Read the texts and answer questions 2 to 5 by yourself. Then discuss your answers with a partner.

2   How are the moongazer and fair maid different from jumbies, according to the information Nichols gives us?

3   Whilst English is the main language spoken in Guyana, the Caribbean people have their own dialect. Identify some examples of this dialect in these texts and write out their Standard English equivalent.

4   *Whole of a Morning Sky* contains a story within a story. Where do the first and second stories begin and end?

5   Do these texts suggest that ghost stories in Guyana are for adults or children – or both? Give reasons for your answer.

Thinking about the text

6   Using the information in the two texts, write an instructional pamphlet for young children entitled 'Warning to children' about the dangers of jumbies in Guyana. Remember to use the features of instructional writing and think carefully about appropriate language for your audience.

7   Jumbie stories are tales passed on orally within the Guyanese culture. Think of an anecdote from your own childhood, make some notes, and then prepare a three-minute oral telling of the tale. Remember to include elements to interest your listener – create an atmosphere, use descriptive language to help them imagine the scene, and consider characters and dialogue.

Night of the Scorpion

Before you read

1   Discuss the following questions in a small group.
    - What does the word 'superstition' mean?
    - Are you a superstitious person?
    - Can you think of any superstitions that are a traditional part of your culture?

2   Consider the words 'night' and 'scorpion'. Jot down all your associations with those two words. Share your ideas with the rest of your class. Are most of the associations positive or negative?

What's it about?

Read the poem and answer questions 3 and 4 by yourself. Then discuss your answers with a partner.

3   The poet describes various things that were tried in order to cure his mother.
    a   List the superstitious rites that are conducted by the local people.
    b   What is the eventual cure?

4   Look again at the final three lines of the poem.
    a   What do these lines show about the mother?
    b   Why do you think the poet chooses to set these out in three simple lines that are separate from the rest of the poem?

Thinking about the text

5   Working in a small group, look at the words below and decide on the three that best describe how the poet portrays the local peasants in this poem. Use evidence from the poem to support your answers.

    superstitious   religious   dangerous   simple   poor

    rich   cruel   interfering   stupid   caring

6   Write your own poem or descriptive piece inspired by your mother or an important female figure in your life. You might like to focus on their overall character, or, as in this poem, tell the story of an incident that illustrates that person's character.

The Long Trial

Before you read

1   Discuss the following questions with a partner:
    - What does the phrase 'sexual equality' mean?
    - What is the balance of equality in the adult partnerships you see in your own life or culture? Are these the same as or different from the way you would want this to be when you are an adult?

What's it about?

Read the story and answer questions 2 to 4 by yourself. Then discuss your answers with a partner.

2   The first four paragraphs establish the setting of the story.
    - What do they tell you about Amina's domestic situation?
    - How do you think the author wants the reader to feel about it? Give reasons for your answer.

3   When Hadj Osman arrived at the house we learn that he is religious and travels to Mecca on pilgrimages. What else does the author tell us about him?

4   Why does Amina give bread to Hadj (page 205)? What does this show about her and what do you think of her actions?

Thinking about the text

5   Look carefully at the language the author uses to describe Amina's viewpoint in the extract below. Write a short paragraph explaining how the language helps us to understand her feelings.

    All around children metamorphosed into grasshoppers, bounded against her, encircled her, transformed her into a clod of earth, inert. Their hundreds of hands became claws, nettles twitching her clothes, tearing her flesh.

6   Consider the title of this story. Write notes on the importance of the title, what the trial is and how it is portrayed in this story. Discuss your ideas in a small group before sharing them with the rest of your class.

The Storyteller's Daughter

Before you read

1   What is your cultural ancestry? How important is this to your own personal identity? Discuss your ideas with the rest of your class.

What's it about?

Read the text and answer questions 2 to 5 by yourself. Then discuss your answers in a small group.

2   What does the first paragraph of the text show about the story-teller's viewpoint of the Afghan capital Kabul? How does the language and imagery convey this?

3   The author refers to her father as an 'alchemist' (page 212). How does the author's language convey a sense of her childhood admiration of his magic?

4   Why do you think the word 'Return' (page 215) is given a capital letter?

5   What does the author feel about her burqa (page 216)?

Thinking about the text

6   In this extract the author emphasises the richness of her Afghan heritage and offers a criticism of the Taliban regime she witnessed in 2001. Make notes on what she admires about Afghanistan and what she is critical of. You might like to organise your notes in two columns.

7   Look at the list of Baghawi of Herat's sayings of the prophet (pages 220–221). Working with a partner, rewrite them in easy-to-read modern English. Then practise and perform a series of tableaux that reflect their meanings.

Compare and contrast

1   Several of the texts in this section consider cultural issues through the eyes of a child. Select three texts that use this technique for comparison. Write notes on the following:
    - who the child is and how this affects the narration of the story
    - the cultural issues the child considers
    - what points the author may be asking the reader to consider.

2   Compare and contrast the portrayal of India in *Film Boy* and *Night of the Scorpion*. You might like to consider the following areas:
    - form of the text
    - purpose of the text
    - the portrayal of poverty
    - the portrayal of wealth
    - author's viewpoint.

3   Compare and contrast two of the portrayals of religion or superstition from the texts in this section. Use the following points to organise your ideas:
    - cultural origin of the text
    - facts about the religion/superstition
    - events described in the text that link to religion
    - the writer's opinion about the religion/superstition and the methods used to convey this to the reader.

4   Choose the opening paragraph of three prose texts from this section. Compare the language and effectiveness of each of them in relation to any of the following areas:
    - preparing the reader for what is to come
    - creating an impact
    - encouraging the reader to read on
    - establishing a narrative voice
    - establishing the setting of the text.

5   Many of the texts in this section consider the role of women in society. Prepare a two-minute speech as part of a hot air balloon debate – you must persuade your audience that your female character is the one who most deserves to stay in the hot air balloon. Work in groups so that each person or pair in your group writes the speech for a different woman.

Notes on authors

Ibrahim Ahmed (1946–) was born in Iraq. He graduated in Law from Baghdad University. He has published several volumes of short stories and a trilogy called *The Child of CNN*. He left Iraq in 1979 and now lives in Sweden.

Simon Armitage (1963–) is one of today's leading UK poets and is also a playwright, travel writer and song lyricist. He lives in Huddersfield. For more information on Simon Armitage and his writing, visit his website at http://www.simonarmitage.co.uk/

Terence Blacker (1948–) was born in Suffolk, England. Most of his books are written for children but he has also written two novels for adults. He is probably best known for his *Ms Wiz* books (Macmillan Children's Books) for younger readers about the adventures of an eccentric teacher. He has written several stories in *Hotshots* (Macmillan Children's Books), a series about an all-girl football team, as well as *The Transfer* (Macmillan Children's Books, 1998), a football story for boys. He also works as a journalist.

Andrée Chedid (1920–) is a poet, dramatist and novelist. Born and educated in Cairo, Egypt, she now lives is Paris. She has won many literary awards including the Prix Goncourt for her short stories and the Prix Mallarmé for poetry.

Jack Cope (Robert Knox) (1913–1991) was a South African novelist, short story writer, poet and editor. He worked in journalism in both South Africa and England and then took up creative writing after he returned to South Africa during World War II. He wrote eight novels, over 100 short stories and several books of poetry. Much of his writing focuses on the political situation of apartheid in South Africa and he was an important literary influence during the 1960s and 1970s.

Nissim Ezekiel (1924–2004) was a poet, playwright and art critic. In his mid twenties he taught English literature at Khalsa College, Mumbai, and published literary articles, before sailing to London and studying philosophy at Birkbeck College. He was considered one of the foremost Indian writers in English of his time.

Zlata Filipović (1980–) is the author of *Zlata's Diary*, a true account of the horrors of the siege of Sarajevo. In 1995 she and her family escaped to Paris. She studied Human Sciences at the University of Oxford and now lives in Dublin. She continues to write.

Nadine Gordimer (1923–) is a South African writer who received the Nobel Prize for Literature in 1991. Much of her writing focuses on the tensions of apartheid in South Africa. She was born into a well-off family in Springs, Transvaal, an East Rand mining town outside Johannesburg. She still lives in South Africa where she continues her work as an author of all kinds of texts including novels, short stories and screenplays.

Krishnan Guru-Murthy (1970–) is a British television newscaster and journalist. He presented the BBC's children's news programme *Newsround* from 1991 to 1994. He has reported on many disasters and conflicts around the world.

Choman Hardi (1974–) was born in Iraqi Kurdistan just before her family fled to Iran. She returned there when she was five, but after chemical weapon attacks on the Kurds when she was 14 her family had to leave once again. Much of her poetry focuses on the issues of flee-ing, survival, fear, family and relationships. The poems included in this anthology were taken from her first collection in English, *Life for Us* (Bloodaxe Books, 2004).

Cassien Mbanda (1984–) was born in Biryogo, Rwanda. At the time of the genocide, he and his family were living in Kigali where his father worked as a driver; his mother was a primary school teacher. Following the genocide, in which he lost both his parents, the organisation Survivors Fund (SURF) helped him rebuild his life.

Alexander McCall Smith (1948–) was born in Rhodesia (now Zimbabwe) and educated there and in Scotland. He is Professor of Medical Law at the University of Edinburgh. His books include works on medical law, criminal law and philosophy, as well as numerous books for children, collections of short stories, and novels.

Geraldine McCaughrean (1960–) was born in London. She has written over 130 books, mainly for children but also some for adults. She has won many literary prizes for her writing. Examples of her prizewinning fiction for children include *A Little Lower than the Angels* (Oxford University Press, 1987), *Plundering Paradise* (Oxford University Press, 1996) and *Gold Dust* (Oxford University Press, 1993). McCaughrean has her own website, where you can find out more about her life and her books:
http://www.geraldine-mccaughrean.co.uk/main.html

Roger McGough (1937–) was born in Liverpool and is a famous British poet. He has even been called the 'patron saint of poetry' by the famous poet Carol Ann Duffy. In the 1960s and 1970s he was part of a group of three famous Liverpool poets called the Mersey Poets. He has his own website, where you can read more of his poetry and find out when he is reading his poetry live around the UK:
http://www.rogermcgough.org.uk

Esther Morgan (1970–) was born in Kidderminster, England. She studied for an MA in Creative Writing at the University of East Anglia. Her first collection, *Beyond Calling Distance* (Bloodaxe Books, 2001), won the 2001 Jerwood Aldeburgh First Collection Prize and was short-listed for the Mail on Sunday/John Llewellyn Rhys Prize. Her second collection is *The Silence Living in Houses* (Bloodaxe Books, 2005). You can find out more about Esther Morgan's life and how she writes poems by looking at her website: http://www.esthermorgan.net

Beverley Naidoo (1943–) was born in South Africa when apartheid was still in place. She protested about this regime from an early age and her writing reflects her disgust at the system. She eventually settled in England. Her first book, *Journey to Jo'burg* (Longman, 1985), won The Other Award in Britain. It focused on children's struggles under apartheid. In South Africa it was banned until 1991, the year after Nelson Mandela was released from jail. For more information about this author see her website:
http://www.beverleynaidoo.com/index2.html

Keiji Nakazawa (1939–) was born in Hiroshima, Japan. He experienced the bombing of Hiroshima and lost many of his family. He eventually became a cartoonist and started working on manga. From 1966 onwards his writing began to focus on the events of Hiroshima, eventually leading to his major work, *Hadashi no Gen*, which was republished in English as *Barefoot Gen* (Project Gen, 1978).

R. K. Narayan (1906–2001) is one of the most famous Indian novelists who wrote in English. Narayan lived to 94, writing for more than 50 years, and publishing until he was 87. He wrote 14 novels, five volumes of short stories, a number of travelogues and collections of non-fiction, condensed versions of Indian epics in English, and the memoir *My Days* (Viking, 1974).

Grace Nichols (1950–) was born in Guyana and grew up in a small coastal village, moving to the city with her family when she was eight. This experience is the basis of her first novel, *Whole of a Morning Sky* (Virago, 1986). Much of her poetry and stories for children reflect her strong interest in Guyanese folk tales, Amerindian myths and the South American civilisations of the Aztec and Inca. She has lived in the UK since 1977 and is married to the poet John Agard.

Frank O'Connor (1903–1966) was an Irish author of over 150 works, best known for his short stories and books of memoirs. He was an only child and his childhood was coloured by his father's alcoholism, poverty and ill-treatment of his mother. From the 1930s to the 1960s he was a prolific writer of short stories, poems, plays and novellas. He also worked as an Irish teacher.

Ken Saro-Wiwa (1941–1995) was a Nigerian businessman, novelist and television producer. His long-running satirical TV series *Basi & Co* was said to be the most watched soap opera in Africa. Saro-Wiwa was a member of the Ogoni people, an ethnic minority whose homelands in the Niger Delta have been targeted for oil extraction since the 1950s. Initially as spokesperson, and then as President, of the Movement for the Survival of the Ogoni People (MOSOP), Saro-Wiwa led a non-violent campaign against environmental damage associated with the operations of multinational oil companies, especially Shell. He was hanged by the Nigerian Military in 1995, along with eight other activists. His death provoked international outrage.

Saira Shah (1964–) was born in London of an Afghan family and brought up in Kent. Her father, now deceased, was Idries Shah, a writer of Sufi fables. Her mother was half Indian and half British. She is a freelance journalist and war reporter.

Norman Silver (1946–) was born in South Africa and now lives in Suffolk. He spent time working in remand homes for teenagers in Bristol and London and is now a full-time writer. Find out more about Norman Silver and read some of his great poems for teenagers at his site: http://www.storybook.demon.co.uk/

Darija Stojnić is from Sarajevo, Bosnia, which was part of the former Yugoslavia. When war broke out in Sarajevo in 1992 she entered England as a refugee. She now works as a counsellor, writer and journalist.

Robert West (1961–1993) spent much of his childhood in and out of remand homes and was ultimately imprisoned on Death Row, in Huntsville, Texas, after murdering DeAnn Klaus in a drunken rage in 1982. According to West, the victim's boyfriend had killed his brother by mistake, intending to kill him. In retaliation, West killed Klaus. All four knew each other and were involved in drug dealing. Robert West was executed on 27 July 1997.

Ken Wiwa (1968–) was born in Nigeria. A journalist and author, he is also well known as the son of Ken Saro-Wiwa. Ken Wiwa has written a book about his father, *In the Shadow of a Saint* (Doubleday, 2000), and he continues his father's work. In 2006, Nigerian President Olusegun Obasanjo appointed Wiwa as special assistant on peace, conflict resolution and reconciliation.